THE HORSE, SAFETY AND THE LAW

Ward Lock Riding School

KNOW YOUR PONY
UNDERSTANDING YOUR HORSE
LEARNING TO RIDE
DISCOVERING DRESSAGE
EVENTING
PRACTICAL SHOWJUMPING
TACK AND CLOTHING
UNDERSTANDING FITNESS AND TRAINING
MODERN STABLE MANAGEMENT

THE HORSE, SAFETY AND THE LAW

VANESSA BRITTON

WARD LOCK

RIDING SCHOOL

WARD LOCK

A WARD LOCK BOOK

First published in the UK in 1994
by Ward Lock
Villiers House
41/47 Strand
London WC2N 5JE

A Cassell Imprint

Distributed in the United States
by Sterling Publishing Co., Inc.
387 Park Avenue South, New York, NY 10016-8810

Distributed in Australia by
Capricorn Link (Australia) Pty Ltd
2/13 Carrington Road, Castle Hill, NSW 2154

British Library Cataloguing-in-Publication Data
A catalogue record for this book is available from the British
Library

ISBN 0-7063-7180-1

Typeset by Litho Link Ltd, Welshpool, Powys, Wales
Printed and bound in Great Britain by Hillman Printers (Frome) Ltd

All photographs by Vanessa Britton

The publishers would like to thank *Your Horse* for permission
to reproduce the contracts on pp 10 and 16.

Frontispiece: Correct signalling for a left turn.

CONTENTS

ACKNOWLEDGEMENTS

My thanks go first to Peter Cannon, Executive Officer, BHS Safety Policy Committee, for commenting on the text. Also to Ceri Jenkins, former BHS Press Officer, for liaising with the various BHS departments on my behalf, and to the staff of the departments themselves who offered information.

I would also like to thank Wendy King, without whose enthusiasm during photo sessions, in a year of few sunny days, the task of illustrating the book would have proved far more difficult. Thanks also to Rosemary Bourne of Equibrand; Andy Pound of animalcare; Mary Awre of MMB Farmkey; Bev Saunders of Safe and Secure Products; and Sue Vincent of Willow End Equestrian Centre and her staff for making the photo sessions at her yard so enjoyable.

INTRODUCTION

RIDING: A RISK SPORT

Anyone who rides a horse should always accept that there is a certain risk involved when doing so. However, some dangers can be minimized by applying a little common sense and following correct safety procedures. Even simply going for a hack in the countryside could prove hazardous if the 'rules' are not adhered to.

While teaching bodies do their best to ensure riders learning under their wing know how to conduct themselves safely, ultimately each individual is responsible for his or her own actions. A momentary loss of concentration, or a lack of consideration for others, could cause an accident.

'It'll never happen to me' is something we are all guilty of thinking, yet accidents will and do happen. The sensible rider always recognizes the risks involved when riding and takes adequate safety precautions against them.

When riding in competitions certain rules and regulations take some of the responsibility off the rider's shoulders. Most shows now insist that all riders on the show-ground wear a hat with a three-point harness to the current British Standards Institution (BSI) standard, and where jumping is to take place

that a body protector is also worn. Every competitor knows the rules and should abide by them if he or she wishes to compete.

Horses are unpredictable animals, however, so anyone who handles them should be prepared for the unexpected; accidents do not only happen to those who ride.

OWNERSHIP: RESPONSIBILITIES

Owning horses is a massive responsibility and yet the pleasure they give to those involved with them far outweighs any burdens they impose.

Horses cost money. They also require complete commitment from their owners. Regular feeding, grooming, riding and healthcare are all necessary to their well-being, and if we choose to own a horse, then we must be prepared to make this commitment to them.

Another responsibility of keeping a horse is ensuring that it does not cause any inconvenience or injury to other people or their property. So, as well as taking care of your horse's needs you should also establish whether you are competent enough to control it, before plunging into ownership.

There are many responsibilities to be undertaken when you decide to

The joy of owning a horse far outweighs any burden of responsibility.

own, look after or ride a horse, so before doing so you need to consider the following.

The horse
Can you say in all certainty that you are always prepared to put your horse before yourself?

Safety
Will you endeavour to be a responsible owner and rider, always taking necessary safety precautions and stopping to think how your actions will affect your own safety, and that of your horse and others?

The law
How, when and where might the law apply to you and how will it affect your life as an owner and/or rider?

CHAPTER 1

BUYING, LEASING OR LOANING A HORSE OR PONY

COSTS AND REQUIREMENTS

Buying a suitable horse will cost a substantial amount of money, yet, in fact, the least expensive part of horse ownership is that initial cost. If buying a sensibly priced, good all-round horse, you can expect to spend at least the same as you paid for it again within the first year, and again every year thereafter.

Horse ownership also costs time and requires a certain degree of knowledge. It is not necessary to be an expert, but you do need to know enough to be able to keep your horse healthy and happy. You should also be able to handle and ride it competently, so as not to put yourself and others at risk.

LEASING

Leasing a horse might involve an initial lease fee, although this should be considerably lower than an outright purchase price. Lease fees vary according to the abilities of the horse. For example, an advanced eventer might be offered for a considerable sum, while an average hacking horse may be offered on a free lease.

A lease usually runs for a certain number of months or years, to be mutually agreed by lessor and lessee. When leasing a horse you will be responsible for its upkeep just as if you were its owner. The drawback to this arrangement, of course, is that when the lease period ends you have had all the expense of upkeep but do not have a horse to show for it.

LOANING

If you are borrowing horses, the maintenance expenses will be the same, although a few owners may agree to share some of the costs. Horses for loan are often referred to as 'meat for manners', where there is no initial fee to pay. This may be of benefit if you can afford regular monthly bills, but not an initial lump sum, or if you only require a horse for a certain period of time.

You should be cautious, however, especially in the absence of a proper agreement, even if the borrower is

This is to certify that (1)...
....
shall be loaned by (2) ....
....
to (3) ....
....
until (4) ....
The horse will be kept at (5) ....
under the following conditions (6)..
and will be used for (7)..
The notice to be given by either party if the horse is to be returned before the
above date is ....
The horse is insured in the sum of £.............. by ....
with the insurance company...
Tack and equipment to be used for this horse are to be provided and kept in good
repair by ....
Vet's, worming and farrier's bills will be paid by......................................

I agree to look after this horse to the best of my ability and to inform its owner immediately should it become lame, ill or otherwise give cause for concern over its welfare, or if it is to be used for any activity other than those stated above.

Signed by borrower .... date..........................
in the presence of..
Signed by the owner...date..........................
in the presence of..

NOTES

1. Name of horse plus brief description including age, height, sex, colour, and any distinguishing features.
2. Name and address of owner.
3. Name and address of borrower.
4. Date at which loan is to be terminated or reviewed.
5. Address at which the horse is to be kept.
6. Whether it will be stabled, turned out, etc.
7. Activities for which the horse is to be used, e.g., showjumping, hunting, breeding, etc.

Suggested loaning contract.

supposedly a good friend. It is important to establish the suitability of the horse for your purpose, and the owner should make known to you any defects or vices that might affect its suitability. For your part, you should only use the horse for the purpose agreed between you, as you are likely to be held responsible for even the slightest degree of negligence, and more so if you were doing something with the horse that was not discussed beforehand.

SHARING

If the expense of keeping a horse is too great for your circumstances, then you could try a horse-share scheme. These can work well if you and your sharer are compatible, but there are some drawbacks. You may not be able to ride when you want or take the horse to the show you want. It is, therefore, important to think all your options through before embarking upon a share arrangement.

EXTRA COSTS OF KEEPING A HORSE

Whether buying, leasing, loaning or sharing you should be aware of both the costs of upkeep and of the demands a horse will make on your time. These include the following.

Vetting

Having decided you want to buy a horse, it is essential to have it vetted. If you do not and it turns out to have some health problem or defect, you might find you have bought a horse which will cost you a great deal more than you thought.

Transport

You will need to find out how much it will cost to bring your new horse home. The previous owner may be able to deliver, usually for a fee, or you might try asking a friend with a horsebox to collect it for you. Failing this, you will need to obtain quotes from transport firms. These will vary depending on distance and whether firms can arrange a shared journey with other customers.

Livery

If you do not have your own land, then you will need to find a suitable livery yard. The cost will vary depending on the type of livery, the facilities at the yard and the area in which you live. These are the types of livery available.

ᘇ *Do-it-yourself*, where you see to all your horse's needs. The cost of a stable will be included if your horse needs to be kept in. A horse that is kept out full-time is known as a grass livery.

ᘇ *Half livery*, where the yard looks after your horse's needs, but you come and ride, and perhaps groom your own horse.

ᘇ *Full livery*, where the yard takes care of your horse completely, including exercising and grooming.

Many yards will also offer schooling and hunting livery services at a higher price.

Feeding

If you intend to keep your horse on do-it-yourself livery, or to keep it at home, you will need to find out how much it will cost to feed it correctly with short feed and hay.

Bedding

The type and cost of bedding you choose will depend on whether your horse needs to be managed in a dust-free environment and so requires a dust-extracted product. More traditional forms of bedding, like straw, are cheaper.

Farriery

Most horses in work require shoeing every five to eight weeks and even if your horse is not to be shod it will still need regular hoof trimming.

Veterinary care

Your horse will need to be vaccinated, have its teeth checked and be wormed regularly. Any unforeseen costs, due to illness or injury for example, will also need to be met.

Lessons

Every rider, whatever their standard, can benefit from having lessons with an experienced instructor, so the cost of tuition should be thought about.

Equipment

Tack, rugs, grooming tools, haynets, a first-aid kit, feed bins, buckets and many other everyday items will all be needed.

11

Insurance

It is a good idea to budget for insurance when considering horse ownership. Most policies cover a certain amount of veterinary fees, and you can choose whether you want to insure against loss of use and tack theft as well. There are various categories of insurance available for the work you will be doing with your horse. Hunter trialing obviously carries a higher injury risk than hacking, and this is reflected in premiums. As a rough guide, premiums work out at about 10 per cent of the horse's value.

Time

Your horse will depend on you to be there for it 365 days a year and it is your duty to keep to a regular routine. Can you offer such a commitment?

BUYING A HORSE

The biggest step towards horse ownership is when you go to see a horse or pony with a view to purchase. Making the wrong decision can cost you dear, whereas the right one will provide you with a friend for a very long time.

The most satisfactory way of buying a horse is through word of mouth. A personal recommendation about a horse or pony for sale can save a lot of searching and disappointments. However, most people do not hear of horses for sale in this way and so buy from advertisements in the equestrian press. The drawback to this is that you know little about the horse before you see it, other than what the seller tells you. Another problem with buying in this way is that you have so little time. You have to make a decision on what you see and what you are told, so to a certain degree you have to have faith in the seller. Unfortunately, many problems may not become apparent until you get your horse home, by which time you may find yourself in a catch-22 situation.

It is clear then that as a potential purchaser you need to be organized, have a clear view of what you want, and need to take all reasonable precautions during viewing and negotiation.

Buying procedure

U Buy a folder and write HORSES FOR SALE on it.

U Make a list of all the things you require your horse to be. (Height, age and abilities, for example.)

U Telephone the seller for further details. Obtain answers to all the questions on your list, and write them down on a piece of paper with the seller's name, address and telephone number on it. Place this in your folder.

U If you are calling in response to an advertisement and decide to go and see the horse, cut out the advertisement and make a note on it of the date you intend to view. Put this in your folder.

U Make arrangements to see the horse.

U Make arrangements to have an experienced horseperson accompany you, as he or she will be able to advise and check out any claims the seller may make.

U Before riding the horse yourself ask to see it ridden.

U If satisfied, ride the horse yourself and have your adviser ride it if possible.

U Observe the horse in its stable for some time and loose in the field if possible.

U Together with your adviser, examine its condition.

U Have the horse vetted, preferably by your own vet, or at least an independent one.

U Examine the vet's certificate and, if necessary, ask the vet to explain any details.

U Ask if you can have the horse for a trial period. Many sellers will not offer this, however, fearing the condition in which the horse might be returned if found unsuitable. So a refusal does not necessarily mean there is something wrong with the horse.

U If you decide to buy the horse, ask for a written warranty from the seller, detailing any specific points, such as 'free from vice' or 'good in traffic'.

U Always obtain a receipt and keep this in your folder. Discard any other papers from the folder that do not concern the horse you

Ask the age of the horse and check it for yourself or have your adviser do so.

Conformation faults

a) Ewe-necked and herring-gutted

b) Hollow-backed with a straight shoulder

c) Roached-back with a bull neck

d) Goose-rumped

have purchased, and put its name on the folder, together with date of purchase.

Viewing

First impressions do count. On arrival at the yard, take a good look round, as the condition of it will often reflect the state of the animals. Even if the buildings are old they should still be bright and tidy. The horses should be alert and in good condition, and the staff or owner helpful.

When viewing a horse you only have a short time to evaluate it, so you should use the time wisely. The seller may try to keep you talking, telling you how good the horse is and what prizes it has won, but you should always be observing the horse.

First, ask to have the horse stood up outside. Take a good look at it. Does it stand quietly? Has it got good conformation? How tall is it?

Ask the horse's age and take a look in its mouth to confirm the answer given or have your adviser do so if you are inexperienced. Ask to have the horse walked and trotted up. Make sure it moves freely and is not lame, and does not have some peculiar action. If you like what you see, ask to have it ridden. Pay particular attention when the horse goes past the gate or towards the field – does it nap? If you want the horse for jumping ask to see it jump a few fences.

If you still like what you see, then ride the horse yourself, and have your adviser ride it if possible. Give the horse a fair trial, remembering you are a stranger. If you will want the horse to jump, then jump it yourself. Always ask to ride the horse on the

roads to see how good it is in traffic.

Having given the horse a fair ridden trial, observe it in the stable. Make sure the seller removes all tack from the door, as this is a common practice to prevent a weaver or crib-biter from showing its trait. Another way of disguising such vices is to feed the horse straight away. Should the seller try this, ask them politely to refrain from doing so. There should be no reason for them to get annoyed at your request, unless something is amiss.

Beware any cover-ups. Is this horse a crib-biter or a weaver?

Dealing with the seller

There are two main benefits of taking an experienced person along with you when viewing a horse. First, your expert can advise on the suitability of the horse and, secondly, they can substantiate anything the seller said to you.

Supposing all has gone well and after listening to your adviser's comments you decide to buy, you should lay a deposit subject to veterinary examination. Five per cent of the asking price is a fair figure, so make sure you have some means of payment with you and always obtain a receipt. While a seller may say they will hold the horse for you, without a deposit they have no obligation to do so. The seller may ask you to come up with the balance within so many days of the veterinary examination, and you should honour this. Whatever agreement is made, always get it in writing.

Making the right decision is extremely important so don't let yourself be rushed or pressurized into buying. An owner might try this by telling you they have someone else coming in ten minutes or that they have already had a good offer for the horse.

Take your time and make your own

Suggested contract of sale.

The seller ....
of...
....(1)
The buyer ....
of...
....(2)
In consideration of the sum of
£........................... today received by the Seller
from the Buyer, the Seller transfers ownership
of the ....
....(3)
named ....to the Buyer and
warrants that the said horse is free from vice
and fit for quiet riding....................................(4).

It is agreed that if the said horse does not comply with any warranty herein contained the Buyer must return it to the Seller at his/her address shown herein not later than

....(5) days
from the date hereof accompanied by a certificate of and signed by a qualified veterinary surgeon specifying in what respect the horse does not comply.

In the event of a dispute as to compliance with any such warranty the horse shall be referred to a qualified veterinary surgeon to be agreed upon by the parties hereto or failing such an agreement nominated by ....

The decision of such veterinary surgeons or arbitrator shall be binding on the parties hereto. As witness the hands of the parties have
this ....199.........(6)
Signed by the seller.......................................(7)
in the presence of ....(8)
Signed by the buyer ....(7)
in the presence of ....(8)

Notes

1. Seller's full name and address.
2. Buyer's full name and address.
3. Brief description of the horse, e.g. bay hunter gelding.
4. Specify any exceptions or qualifications to the warranty, e.g. 'except that he shies at loud or sudden noise' or any additional warranties given.
5. State the number of days within which the horse must be returned. Seven days would usually be the maximum.
6. Insert the actual date of the agreement.
7. Seller's and buyer's signatures respectively.
8. Witness should sign here and insert his/her address and occupation.

General notes

This agreement should be signed by both parties in duplicate so that each has a copy for future reference. It is recommended that a certificate by a qualified veterinary surgeon should be obtained by the buyer before entering into any agreement.

This agreement is suitable for the usual sale and purchase of a horse for riding. However, if there are special circumstances or exceptional warranties, you should take specialist advice or have the agreement drawn up by your solicitor.

decision. If you need convincing that this is the horse for you, then it almost certainly isn't. Do not be afraid to say no.

Be polite and thank the seller for their time, but you don't need to keep making apologies and you don't have to justify your decision. That the horse is not right for you is fair enough.

Buying from a dealer

While many people are wary of buying from professional dealers, you receive additional protection in law if you do so. For example, if you inform the dealer that you want the horse as a show-jumper, and after purchase the horse refuses to jump, you can claim against the dealer. However, if the dealer advised you that the horse was not suitable for jumping, but you liked it and bought it anyway, you would have no redress. Nor would the dealer be liable if you were informed of any specific defect which subsequently proved to hinder the horse.

In the past dealers were thought of as being 'shady characters' who might 'rip you off', but in the main this image is unfair today.

Most dealers are fair, and honestly try to match horse and purchaser to the best of their ability. If the horse proves unsuitable the dealer will exchange it for another without quibble. After all, dealers have a reputation to uphold.

If word gets around that they are untrustworthy they will soon start to lose business, and they are also hoping that you might come back to them when you are looking to buy another horse.

Buying from an auction

The ancient rule of *caveat emptor* (let the buyer beware) is still the best advice to heed today, especially if buying from sales. It can be a tricky business as you need experience and the ability to judge a horse from appearance. The catalogue may not tell you very much and this is often intentional. If something is not stated the seller or auctioneers cannot be held liable. However, you also need to know what is meant by what *is* mentioned. Here is some jargon of the trade which is meant to impress the less experienced.

ꙶ If the horse has any good virtues the catalogue will try to emphasize these. Good to box, shoe, clip or good in traffic are all good selling points, so if they are not mentioned the horse is probably not good in these respects.

ꙶ If the catalogue says 'has' jumped or 'has' driven, then you can take it that the horse either has not for a long time, did not like it or was not very good at it.

ꙶ 'Believed' is a commonly used word. It could mean the owners have never witnessed what is believed, or that they know it not to be true, but think such a statement could add to the horse's value. Believed sound and believed quiet in all respects are common phrases. Beware!

ꙶ 'Potential' is also a favourite word among sellers. It implies that the horse may have ability in a certain discipline were it to be tried at that discipline. However, the seller almost certainly has not tried it, so does not know whether the horse has the ability or not. Proven ability can be substantiated by money won or points gained through the various governing bodies of the relevant sport, and these can be checked.

U 'Will make' an eventer or a dressage horse is a phrase that is often seen. Who says so? It is only an opinion and you are better off relying on your own instincts than those of the seller.

The buyer who bears in mind that many sellers exaggerate the good and forget to mention the bad is the most likely to purchase a suitable horse. That is not to say you should never consider an unwarranted horse; only that if you do you should also consider the price you pay accordingly.

If the auctioneer states something verbally about the horse that is not mentioned in the catalogue, then you have some comeback if what they say proves to be false, whether it is written down in the catalogue or not.

Study the conditions of sale very carefully and make sure you fully understand what does or does not constitute a warranty; how long any warranty period lasts; and any conditions under which a warranty does not apply: e.g. horses sold under a certain price or sold privately before they go through the ring, or even horses without a full set of shoes!

You are generally entitled to return a horse bought at auction if a problem arises which contravenes what the catalogue stated or what the auctioneer said. You should confirm at the time of purchase how many days you have in which to inform the auctioneers of misdescription or breach of warranty. You will have no redress if you return the horse outside any specified time limit.

Veterinary certificates and warranties

While a veterinary certificate provides evidence of a horse's soundness, it does not guarantee that the horse has no faults. It is a sensible precaution, therefore, to ask the seller for a written warranty covering things already confirmed verbally, for instance, that the horse is free from vice, that it is easy to shoe and box, and that it is sensible in traffic. The warranty should also provide evidence of performance, money won or points obtained, for example.

Once you are totally satisfied that the horse is the one you want, pay the balance and obtain a receipt of purchase for your folder.

WHAT TO DO IF THINGS GO WRONG

What should you do if, after you have had the horse home for a while, you find it is not suitable for your purpose?

First, you should contact the seller, explain the trouble and try to come to

Buying from sales or auctions can be a tricky business as they are ideal places for other people's cast-offs.

some sort of amicable agreement. You could discuss whether (a) they would be prepared to take the horse back and refund your money; (b) take the horse back and exchange it for another; or (c) refund part of your money.

If no agreement can be reached you should contact an experienced equestrian solicitor, who will advise on the likelihood of success in establishing liability.

If the horse proves unsuitable it may also be that you can hold the vet who produced the veterinary certificate liable in negligence if the vet either (a) failed to spot a fault which undoubtedly must have been present at the time of examination; or (b) the horse had a permanent problem which must have been present at the time of examination. Again, you should contact a solicitor experienced in equestrian law to act for you when pursuing any claim.

LAWS AND LIABILITIES

In law, disputes between buyer and seller are civil matters. This means they have to be decided on a balance of probabilities, which can often mean whose evidence is accepted.

Misrepresentation arises if you bought a horse on the basis of what the seller told you, or what an advertisement said about a horse, and it subsequently turned out to be false. To bring a successful claim you will need to prove that the seller did not have grounds for believing what they said was true. If you are successful, you will be entitled to a full refund or to compensation for misrepresentation.

Breach of contract is similar, but is considered in the light of whether the false statement is a major or minor one, and compensation will be awarded accordingly. The word 'warranted' on the contract does not guarantee anything but the horse's soundness, unless extra factors are stated afterwards.

INSURANCE

Ideally you should arrange insurance cover from the moment you hand over your money to the seller, or from the moment the hammer falls at a sale, when you legally become the horse's owner. This is easy if you are buying from a private person or a dealer, as you will have a few days in which to arrange cover before collection. However, if buying from a sale you should inform your insurers that you might be purchasing a horse and ask about cover from the fall of the hammer. Remember, if a horse you have bought gets injured when being led from the ring to the box, it is your problem.

The importance of having a receipt for the sum paid also applies when you come to insure the horse. If you buy a horse for £2,000 and you have a receipt to prove it, you will have no trouble in insuring the horse for this sum. You will also be paid the full £2,000 if your horse is killed in an accident, if it is put down to prevent further suffering or if its injuries prevent it from carrying out the job you bought it for, providing you take out the correct cover.

CHAPTER 2

HANDLING HORSES

COMMON SENSE

It is not necessary to be an expert to handle horses safely, but you do need to apply a little common sense to all situations and above all you should be prepared to learn. While your friends may be willing to help you, a lot can also be learned from your horse. We all learn by our mistakes and, in the case of handling a horse safely, we learn with lightning speed. A half-ton horse on your toe soon speeds up the learning process. However, there are four basic rules to remember when handling a horse:

- speak gently;
- move steadily and quietly;
- be gentle, but firm;
- always think before acting.

You should always stop and think about what effect your actions will have, before carrying them through. Learning a little horse psychology will also help you to anticipate and understand your horse's actions and moods. A horse learns by repetition, so to make your job of handling it easier, you should carry out the necessary tasks routinely, until they become second nature to it. For example, if you pick your horse's feet out every time you bring it in, or on leaving the stable, it will soon

anticipate your moves and will be ready to lift its hoof at the appropriate time.

Your horse's expressions will tell you much about it.

a) A quiet and happy horse

b) A very angry horse

Your horse's eye is also a great aid to handling it safely. By studying its eye you will soon begin to know its moods, likes and dislikes. It will be easy for you to see whether it is calm or anxious.

Thus, to create a safe environment for your horse you need to learn how to carry out tasks correctly, and you also need to get to know your horse as an individual, respecting its own needs, likes and dislikes.

HANDLER'S REQUIREMENTS

To have a good and happy association with horses, you will need three attributes. The first is confidence, for if the horse is allowed to realize that it is much stronger than you, it will try to take advantage by pulling you around. You must therefore be confident when attending the horse and instil some discipline to gain the horse's respect. This is the only way you can hope to manage it safely.

The second is an ability to learn. While we all have to learn the basics at first, we should also endeavour continually to progress. 'You never stop learning' is a true saying.

The third is competency. You need to be able to handle and ride/drive the horse correctly, if you are to do so safely.

SAFETY PROCEDURES

When *approaching the horse* you should do so quietly and calmly, informing it of your presence by talking to it. It is safest to approach towards the horse's head from the side for two reasons. First, this way it can see you coming and will not be startled and, secondly, the horse will not be able to kick out at you or swing its quarters round and barge into you.

While you might think you know your horse, you should never become complacent, as even a horse with the mildest nature can become scared for no apparent reason and act out of character.

When *leading your horse* there are three things to remember in the interests of safety. First, you should always wear gloves, if possible, as lead ropes can cause nasty burns if pulled

This is how the horse sees, which is why you should approach it from the front and slightly to the side.

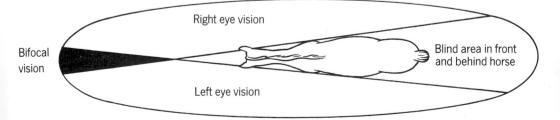

Leading the horse correctly.

quickly through the fingers. Secondly, you should think about where you are leading your horse. If in the company of other horses or on the roads, lead your horse in a bridle for more control. Thirdly, you should ensure you are holding the rope correctly. If leading from the nearside (in traffic you should lead from the offside – see Chapter 7), your right hand should be held close to the clip, with your left hand taking up the slack of the rope. You should never wrap the lead rope around your hand, as this could result in you being dragged or at best receiving an extremely nasty burn.

When *leading the horse on the roads at dusk* or in dull conditions, always wear something that shows up in poor light, preferably a reflective tabard.

The horse should also wear reflective legbands and a reflective headcollar. You can also wear a light on your arm, showing white to the front and red to the rear, to inform other traffic that you are there, from a distance.

When *turning your horse* you should push it away from you and turn in a fairly large circle, always keeping yourself on the outside.

Tying up your horse incorrectly is a major safety hazard. One of the first things any horseowner should learn is how to tie a quick-release knot. In an emergency the horse can then be freed quickly. For added safety, a length of string or bailer twine (not nylon) should be attached to the tethering ring, and this will break if the horse pulls back when in danger.

23

How to tie a quick-release knot.

Where the horse is tied will also affect its safety. It should not be tied up in an open space, from where, if it were to break free, it could run into open fields or out on to a road. The ring on to which the horse is tied should be fixed to a secure object, such as a wall or gate-post, which will not give way before the string breaks, should the horse panic and pull back.

When *turning your horse out*, turn its head towards the gate before letting it go, to prevent you from being kicked if it suddenly decides to display some high spirits!

When *grooming*, tie your horse fairly short to prevent it from moving about or from becoming caught up in the rope. Keep all your grooming utensils in a grooming tray and leave it out of the way of the horse's feet, and your own. When brushing the horse's tail stand to the side so that you cannot easily be kicked.

When *picking out a hoof*, don't just try to snatch it up as the horse may whip it up so quickly that it hits you in the face. While speaking to your

horse, run your hand down its shoulder and leg, until you come to below its fetlock joint. Gently squeeze and say 'Up boy/girl'. Once the horse lifts its foot, support it at

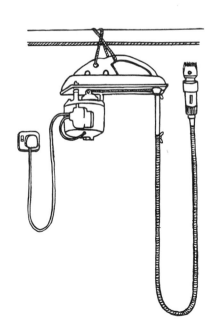

Clippers on a pulley system.

the toe with your other hand. If this procedure is followed every time the horse is required to pick its feet up, it will soon become an easy task.

When brushing mud from the coronet or oiling your horse's hooves, you should crouch down so that you can jump out of the way quickly if necessary. If you kneel or sit on the floor you might not be able to escape quickly enough and could be trampled if your horse becomes startled.

When *clipping*, do not tie your horse up but have an assistant hold it. Ensure that the clipper blades are sharp, well oiled and free from dirt. The cable should be on a pulley system, or at least away from where the horse could tread on it or become tangled up. To ensure that your horse does not get a bad shock if it does get tangled up, employ a circuit breaker or have a 12-V converter fitted.

When *rugging*, all three basic handling rules apply. You also need

Dealing with youngsters can be hazardous if you do not take the necessary safety precautions.

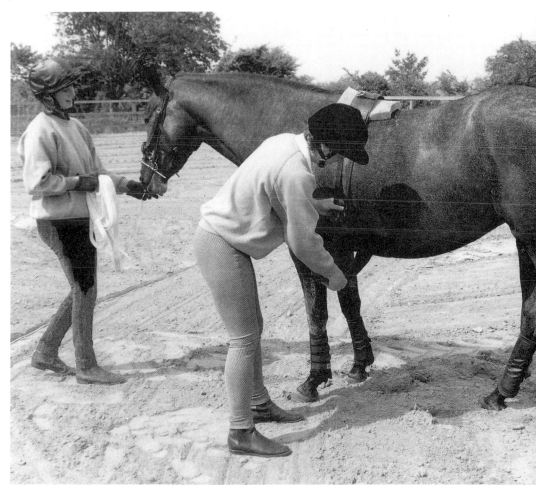

to ensure the rug fits the horse well and is adjusted comfortably. When fitting the rug don't throw it wildly over your horse's back as this may frighten it.

Many owners will tie a horse up *while it is being shod*, but it is safer if you can hold it.

While holding it you will be able to judge its reactions to the farrier and can soothe it if it seems a little nervous. You can also move it one way or another as required by the farrier.

Similarly when *being seen by a veterinary surgeon*, the horse may need soothing or moving.

Special care

Some horses need special care when being handled. A youngster may be nervous or boisterous, either of which may put your safety at risk, so you will need to be extra careful.

It is essential that a young horse is taught the basics as early in life as possible, before it gets too big to handle.

The horse should be taught how to be led, tied up, how to move over, accept being groomed or rugged, and to respect its handler at all times.

An old or ill horse will also need special handling, with a little extra loving care. You should allow such a horse to walk at its own pace. The horse might also want a little bit of fussing or it may need to be left alone to rest.

You should also bear in mind that a feeble horse may fall against you if it stumbles or loses its balance, so you must take the necessary measures to prevent yourself from also becoming a casualty.

RESPONSIBLE USE OF EQUIPMENT

Equipment for horses is costly and so needs to be treated with respect. Many items can also be potentially dangerous, so they should be handled with care. Always read the manufacturer's instructions that come with the equipment carefully and, if you are inexperienced, try to practise on an older, calm horse, before tackling a younger, more novice one.

When using electrical items, ensure that the plug and your hands are dry, and that the appliance itself does not get wet, unless designed to do so. Also, always fit a circuit breaker to prevent accidental shocks.

Yard tools should be used responsibly and put away safely. A fork or rake thrown down is simply waiting for someone to come along and stand on it, and whack themselves in the face.

Electric groomers are excellent if used sensibly and are a great aid to a groom in charge of many horses. Remember that new horses will need to be introduced to the machines slowly and that unfortunately some horses will never accept them, however much you persevere.

Many grooming machines work in the same way as a vacuum cleaner; others have revolving brush heads, either of a body brush or dandy brush density. It is extremely important that these heads do not come into contact with the horse's mane or tail as they will tangle up in them and pull the hair. In fact, it is best if the tail is bandaged, therefore, and the mane clipped up with hairdressing clips or tied up with rubber bands.

Always remember that the horse is in your care. If you leave an electrical cable trailing across the yard and your horse treads on it, then you have only yourself to blame.

INSURANCE

Handling your horse safely will cut down on any injuries, but inevitably accidents will happen, so insurance to cover the unforeseen is a sensible, if not essential, precaution. While having insurance is not yet a legal requirement, it is actually as important to a horse owner as to the motorist. A horse represents a great investment to most people and should therefore be insured as quickly as possible after purchase.

Most insurance companies offering horse insurance set out standard policies, with varying degrees of risk. The greater the risk involved the higher the premium will be. The general riding horse will be cheaper to insure than the advanced eventer, for example. However, if your requirements do not fall into a standard category then you should enquire about a tailor-made policy to suit your purpose. Any rider/driver should consider taking out insurance to cover the following important areas.

∪ *Veterinary fees* Usually these will be insured up to a maximum price, depending on the policy and risk factor. You should ensure that the quoted cover is not limited to a percentage of the sum insured, but is the sum which you will receive per claim. You usually have to pay the first part ('the excess') of any claim. If you want

your horse to receive complementary treatments, such as hydrotherapy, physiotherapy or homoeopathy, you should check that your policy covers this.

∪ *Personal accident* This covers you or any person riding/driving your horse with your permission in the event of an accident. Some policies also offer cover for temporary or total disablement, immediate hospital cash or dental cover.

∪ *Mortality* This should cover full replacement value if your horse unfortunately dies or has to be put down. Check whether the insurers require you to inform them before putting a horse down, because such requirements can prolong unnecessary suffering. Some policies do not cover a horse for a general anaesthetic, unless undergoing a lifesaving operation, so you should find one that does.

∪ *Third party liability* Lack of third party liability could prove very expensive and so is really essential to every person who keeps a horse. Damages soon add up. Just imagine if your horse got loose on the roads, ran into someone's garden, smashed up his greenhouse, trampled his roses . . . Could your bank balance cover it without insurance? Remember that every fully paid-up member of the British Horse Society is covered for personal liability, up to £2 million of cover for any one claim, in respect of using a horse or horse-drawn vehicle.

27

∪ *Saddlery and tack* Tack theft is increasing at an alarming rate, so you should make sure it is covered by your policy and for damage too.

∪ *Immediate cover* Some policies do not commence cover for 30 days, which is obviously unacceptable. If you have a credit card it is possible to insure your horse from the moment you purchase it.

∪ *Loss of use* This does not mean that the horse can no longer be used, but that it can longer be used for the purpose it was bought for. For example, the horse might be saved from death by veterinary technology, but it may not be fit to resume a hectic competitive life. So, it is important to decide what you intend to use the horse for and therefore insure accordingly. If the horse is only insured for light hacking and dressage, and gets injured in a cross-country event, you will not be covered.

Which policy?

To start with you could ask your veterinary surgeon to recommend an insurance company, since vets have to fill in many forms relating to equestrian claims, and generally have a good idea about which ones give a prompt and helpful service. A horse-owning friend or colleague, or your riding school, might also be able to give a personal recommendation.

When considering insurance without a personal recommendation, it is a good idea to shop around as some insurers are priced more competitively than others, and some

policies are fairer than others. The most expensive quotation does not always mean you will get the best cover. However, there is no point in settling for a policy that does not meet all your requirements, simply because you will save money in the short term.

When choosing insurance make a list of your needs and ensure that they are covered by the policy. Read *all* the small print and, if you are unsure on any point, ring the company and ask to have it explained clearly. If you don't check the small print you might find when it comes to claiming that you are not covered because of a minor detail.

In particular, check what exclusions there are for vet's fees, public liability and for tack. Also make sure if you ride someone else's horse that they have insurance and you are covered for public liability. Many insurers cover an additional named rider, aged between 5 and 65, quite cheaply.

Realizing that insurance is essential does not make it any easier to pay, so many insurance companies now accept monthly or quarterly instalments to spread the costs.

Cover for non-owners or riders

A common misconception is that most horse-related injuries occur from falls. In fact, you are just as likely to incur an injury off a horse as on it. Common injuries result from bites, kicks, being squashed against the stable wall and being stood on. It makes sense, then, to have a policy that covers any injuries experienced while handling the horse, as well as when riding or driving.

CHAPTER 3

THE HORSE AT GRASS

FENCING

Basically, a fence is used to keep a horse inside a paddock, so it obviously needs to be high enough to prevent it from jumping over. You should also make sure that any fence is not so low that the horse can trap its foot between the fence and the ground; that it is strong enough to prevent the horse from pushing it over, should it rub on it or accidentally run into it; and that it is clearly visible to the horse so that it does not run straight into it.

Various types of fencing materials are used and some are safer than others.

Natural enclosures
These include trees, hedges and ditches. Trees on their own are not secure enough for horses, as they will simply walk through any gaps.

From a safety point of view natural hedges make excellent field boundaries. They prevent cuts and nasty injuries, but you should remember that in winter foliage may be sparse which could provide the horse with a means of escape. Hedges also need to be high enough to prevent the horse from jumping out, should it so desire. It is therefore sensible to take extra security measures and place safe fencing in

front of the hedge to prevent such occurrences in wintertime.

While horses are sometimes enclosed by ditches, these are not particularly safe. They need to be deep enough and wide enough to deter horses from jumping across them, or walking into and out of them. However, serious problems can occur if one horse is chased into this type of ditch by other horses.

Post and rail
Post and rail has always been considered the best fencing for horses. It is strong, clearly visible and safe. Either two or three rails can be used, depending on whether large horses or smaller ponies are kept in the field. To ensure strength there should not be more than a 1.8 m (6 ft) span between posts. The posts themselves should be 13 cm by 7.5 cm (5 in by 3 in), or 10 cm by 10 cm (4 in by 4 in), and should be dug about 60 cm (2 ft) into the ground, and back-filled so that the fencing will 'give' in an emergency and not snap under pressure. They should be treated with creosote to protect them from winter weather.

Make sure that gates are sited in the centre of the fencing. If they are in the corner of the field horses can get trapped and bullied at bringing in or feeding time.

Post and rail is the safest fencing for horses, with the gate in the centre.

Stud rails can also be used instead of traditional wooden rails. They are made up of lengths of high-tensile wire, covered with a 10 cm (4 in) wide band of plastic. They need very little maintenance and are quite safe. Any sharply angled corners should be railed across to prevent the horse from becoming trapped or injured on them.

Wire fencing

Whether barbed, plain-line wire, sheep netting or electric fencing, all wire fencing can cause horrific injuries to horses and is best avoided.

Security

To prevent the horse from escaping or being stolen always make sure gates are closed and padlocked at both ends. If possible, site the gate away from any road entrance and in view of the house or stables.

Alarms can be fitted to the gate, so that if it is opened a noise will sound wherever the receiver is sited, usually in the house.

PASTURE MANAGEMENT

The condition of your horse's grazing land is very important for three main reasons. First, it provides the horse with food in the form of grass. Secondly, it provides an exercise area. And thirdly, it provides as near 'natural' conditions for the horse as it is likely to get as a domesticated animal and so benefits its mental state.

Horse pasture needs maintenance from time to time, depending on the amount of horses grazing the area, on the time of year and on the weather.

Generally, a well-maintained pasture of about 2 hectares (5 acres) will support five horses, but 0.4

hectare (1 acre) alone will not support one horse. To keep such a pasture in good condition you should sub-divide it into three sections and employ a rotation system. Each section will then receive a period of grazing, a period of treatment and a period of rest. To help maintain any pasture in good condition, whether sub-divided or not, you should:

ᴜ pick up droppings regularly;

ᴜ top the field (cut long grass) throughout the growing season, especially if the grass becomes longer than 15 cm (6 in);

ᴜ lightly harrow the field in hot, dry conditions after dung removal, to remove dead grass and aerate the soil, and to clear up the paddock at the end of the summer;

ᴜ rest the field periodically, if possible, to allow regrowth;

ᴜ while horses are off the pasture treat with a herbicide to destroy unwanted vegetation, if necessary;

ᴜ fertilize (or top dress) to encourage strong, new growth, but consult manufacturer's

Paddocks should be lightly harrowed to aerate the soil and encourage regrowth.

recommendations on when to allow horses back into the paddock, since different products require varying amounts of time;

◡ try to introduce mixed grazing with sheep or cattle, as horses and other stock complement each other's grazing patterns, and can also help with worm control, since when sheep or cattle ingest worm larvae from horses they will not survive and vice versa.

Drainage

Good drainage is important as it prevents the field from becoming 'poached' (boggy) in wet conditions. Natural drainage is provided by a field with a gentle slope running into a ditch at the bottom. Sandy fields will also drain better than clay, so soil type plays an important part. If the land becomes particularly wet and boggy each year, put some fine shale in front of gates and around the water trough to prevent horses standing in wet, sloppy mud for long periods.

As mud dries, it will form hard ruts from the horse's hoof prints, so just before it becomes hard baked, the land should be rolled to flatten it out. Otherwise horses can strain themselves or trip up on the ruts.

Poisonous plants

When considering the care of your horse's pasture you should be aware of what is growing in it. While the growth of certain grasses is to be encouraged, weeds and poisonous plants must be eradicated. The most common plants that are poisonous to horses are ragwort (*Senecio jacobaea*), bracken (*Pteris aquilina*), yew (*Taxus baccata*) and oak (*Quercus*).

Some other more common poisonous plants include: *Rhododendron*; foxglove (*Digitalis purpurea*); laburnum (*Laburnum vossii*); deadly nightshade (*Atropa belladonna*); and the leaves and stems of potatoes or green potatoes themselves. Other poisonous plants to be found in the UK are: hemlock (*Conium maculatum*); laurel (*Prunus laurocerasus*); privet (*Ligustrum ovalifolium*); horsetail (*Equisetum arvense*); poppy (*Papaver rhoeas*); lupin (*Lupinus*); buttercup (*Ranunculus*); chickweed (*Stellaria media*); black nightshade (*Solanum nigrum*); black bryony; (*Tamus communis*); flax (*Linum*); buckthorn (*Rhamnus carthartica*); darnel (*Lolium temulentum*); alder buckthorn (*Alnus cordata*); hellebore (*Helleborus*); lily-of-the-valley (*Convallaria majalis*); columbine (*Aquilegia vulgaris*); henbane (*Hyoscyamus niger*); *Iris*; St John's wort (*Hypericum*); bog asphodel (*Narthecium ossifragum*); pimpernel (*Anagallis*); broom (*Cytisus*); white bryony; (*Bryonia cretica*); thorn apple (*Datura stramonium*); sowbread (*Cyclamen purpurascens*); monkshood (*Aconitum napellus*); greater hemp (*Galeopsis*); *Fritillaria*; soapwort (*Saponaria officinalis*); sandwort (*Arenaria*); larkspur (*Delphinium*); white celandine (*Chelidonium*); corn cockle (*Agrostemma githago*); meadow saffron (*Colchicum autumnale*); herb Paris (*Paris quadrifolia*); cowbane (*Cicuta virosa*); hemlock water dropwort (*Oenanthe crocata*); and the bulbs of daffodil (*Narcissus*), hyacinth (*Hyacinthus*), snowdrop (*Galanthus nivalis*) and bluebell (*Hyacinthoides non-scripta*).

Ragwort   Acorns   Yew

Rhododendron   Foxglove   Bracken

Laburnum   Deadly nightshade   Potato (green potatoes, leaves and stems)

Some poisonous plants.

Some plants can have fatal consequences, while others may only cause mild poisoning or have a cumulative effect. For instance, ragwort has a cumulative effect and is likely to cause the most trouble, especially where grass is sparse. Horses will normally avoid it unless there is little else for them to eat. It also becomes more palatable after being sprayed, when it is wilting, so horses are in danger at these times. It can also cause poisoning if it has been cut and baled in hay.

Once it has flowered ragwort is clearly visible because of its bright yellow flowers. However, it is safer if it can be removed while still in its early growth, characterized by a dense rosette of leaves low to the ground.

If poisoning is suspected – for example, if the horse is seen behaving oddly, perhaps showing colicky signs, acting excitedly, or convulsing – a veterinary surgeon must be called immediately.

Injurious Weeds Act 1959

The Ministry of Agriculture, Fisheries and Foods (MAFF) has powers to serve clearance notices regarding certain injurious weeds on an owner or occupier of land. So, not only do horseowners have a duty to ensure their horses are safe from poisoning, but they also have a duty to comply with the law.

Prevention is always better than cure, so every horseowner should regularly check the horse's paddock, and remove and burn anything that is, or even may be, poisonous. 'If in doubt, pull it out!' Poisonous trees should be fenced off so that no horse can reach them and to prevent any produce (acorns, for example) falling into the field.

Poisonous plants should be fenced off.

Watering systems

A self-filling, galvanized water trough is ideal for horses, although very few people have the resources to install these. Other systems can be employed which are just as safe and more economical. For example, an old bathtub can be used as a water trough, although it must have its taps removed and should be panelled up to the top, to prevent the horse from trapping or injuring its legs. Water troughs should be placed near to a water supply, so regular cleaning, which is essential, can be carried out with the minimum of effort.

Natural water supplies are provided by streams or rivers, although there are safety factors to consider here. There should be an easy approach to a gravelled bottom, with running water. A sandy or muddy-bottomed stream is not suitable, nor is one with steep or crumbling banks.

Ponds, unless the bottom is also gravelled and is fed by a spring or stream with a firm approach, are not suitable water sources either, as they may be stagnant or polluted. These must be fenced off and an alternative water supply provided.

Grazing horses together

A group of horses grazing together usually settles well, after an initial inquisitive period, if all the horses are put into a field at the same time. Problems can occur when a new horse is introduced, so this should be done gradually. If possible the new horse should be turned out into a paddock adjacent to the one containing the other horses. The other horses will then be able to get used to the new horse, without hurting it. After a few

Unsuitable ponds should be fenced off.

then be put back with the main group. This method usually causes few arguments between the horses.

The new field

Before turning any horses out into an unknown field you should check that there are no hidden dangers, such as chain harrows or rollers lying about in long grass. You should also check for discarded rubbish and broken bottles, especially if the field has a right of way through it.

days one of the established group should be put in with the new horse. A few days later these two should

You should also check whether the fencing is safe and secure, whether the water source is safe and clean, and whether there are any poisonous weeds or plants growing in the field.

An old bathtub is a safe watering system as long as it is panelled up and has had the taps removed.

WORMING

Worming is one of the horseowner's biggest responsibilities. Neglecting to worm your horse will lead to illness and, in some cases, death. The responsible owner will worm every six to ten weeks, depending on individual circumstances, such as whether the horse is stabled, at grass, in poor condition or kept with others, for instance.

Horses play host to many various types of worm and it may be necessary to treat them with different wormers, manufactured to kill individual types of worm, from time to time. Your vet can advise which brand to use if a certain type of worm infestation is suspected.

Worming is a simple and effective process. You can buy worming powders to add to the horse's feed or you can by a tube of paste that is squirted into the horse's mouth. Your veterinary surgeon will be able to offer advice on which method to use.

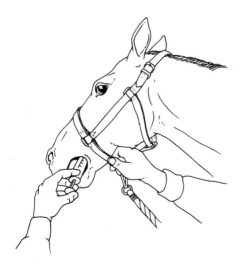

Administering worming paste by syringe.

To help prevent worm infestation remove dung from paddocks frequently. Also remove bot-fly eggs from the horse (seen as little yellow specks around the backs of the legs, chest and neck) as soon as they appear.

WINTERING OUT

A horse living out in the winter will need to keep warm. Some heavier breeds will grow a sufficient coat to provide all the warmth they need. Other finer breeds, such as Thoroughbreds, will probably need rugging with a waterproof rug, known as a New Zealand rug.

Any rug used should be designed so that it rights itself after rolling. For this purpose many rugs are now quite deep and do not have a surcingle, only crossover straps which go around the horse's hind legs. These straps should not sag down below the hock, or the horse may get its leg caught in the strap when lying down.

Horses also need shelter from driving rain and wind. If there are no high natural hedges sheltering the field, then a field shelter should be erected. This should be put up with the back of the shelter taking the brunt of the prevailing wind. The back should either butt up against the fence so that a horse cannot get trapped between the shelter and the fence, or should be far enough away from any fence to allow easy access behind.

A single shelter (designed for one horse) can have an open front. A shelter for more than one horse should have an entrance and an exit, to allow escape from a bullying horse if necessary.

A well-fitting New Zealand rug will afford the finer wintered-out horse some protection. Note how the hind leg-straps are crossed over.

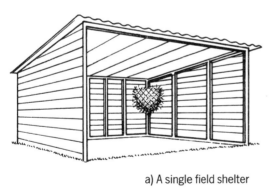

a) A single field shelter

b) A double field shelter

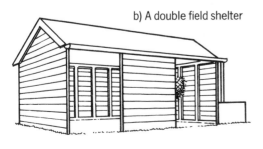

ACQUIRING A REGISTERED FARRIER

The best way to acquire a good farrier is by personal recommendation from a horseowner. Good farriers are hard to come by, so it helps if you can arrange to have your horse shod, along with others, at a neighbouring yard. Avoid farriers who are always advertising, as good farriers should have more than enough business without doing so. Ask your friends a few questions about their horses' farrier. Do their horses frequently lose shoes? Do they go lame after being shod, or play up while being shod? If the answer is yes to any of these questions ask other people who use the farrier the same questions.

If you do not know anyone who can recommend a suitable farrier, obtain a list of registered farriers from the Farriers Registration Council.

37

STRAYING

An escaped horse, after its initial excitement at being free, will probably head for the nearest field of green grass – or crops. As this land will almost certainly belong to someone else, your horse will be trespassing.

If the horse causes damage while trespassing you will be expected to pay compensation, so make sure you are insured for this. Your insurers will certainly investigate whether your neighbour's land was fenced securely and if it was not they may fight the claim.

However, a horse need not even escape from its own field to trespass. If your horse sticks its head into the garden next door and starts to eat apples off your neighbour's trees it is trespassing. If by doing so the horse manages to break the fence then it is your responsibility to replace it or pay for repair.

LAWS AND LIABILITIES

You will be aware that if you own or look after a horse for someone else, you have an obligation to look after its welfare and health as if it were your own. However, whether you are simply its keeper, or its owner, you also have further obligations. You should be aware of the effect your horse's actions may have on other people, their property or animals. Horses can cause damage to other people's property if they stray on to it, or they might cause injury to a person or other animal. As the horse's keeper (which in law means either an owner or a person in possession of someone else's horse), you will be held responsible, in most cases, for any harm or damage that occurs as a result of its actions.

While many people might overlook a slight nuisance, such as finding a stray horse on their land, they are likely to be less understanding if a great deal of damage or injury has occurred. As a result, they are almost certain to make a claim directly against you, or perhaps in some cases under their own insurance policy, and this is where the question of responsibility arises. Most claims are made for damage to motor vehicles or to farmers' crops or for substantial personal injury.

Responsibility in the eyes of the law

If you are the keeper of a horse who has caused damage or injury, you are likely to be the person held responsible for its actions, whether you were present at the time of the incident or not. However, sometimes the person in charge of a horse at the time of the injury or damage will be the one held responsible. Where an owner is under 16 years of age, responsibility may lie with the parents or guardians.

In the case of personal injury, certain factors will be considered which will help to determine responsibility. For example, did you take all reasonable care when riding or leading your horse, or when leaving it unattended?

If the injured party were to establish a case against you, by producing evidence that you did not in fact take all reasonable care, you could be sued for negligence.

U Was your horse totally out of your control when it caused the injury?

U Were you aware that your horse had some peculiar habit which was the cause of the injury?

U Was it inevitable that your horse was likely to cause damage, whether you had control of it or not?

If you admitted that the answers would be 'yes' to the above questions, then you would almost certainly be held responsible for your horse's actions and the injured party could sue you. On the other hand, you may be able to ask whether the person voluntarily accepted the risk of injury. For example, did they enter your stable or field having ignored a warning sign against doing this? If so, any injury caused as a result may be deemed to be their own fault.

It may be a similar outcome if they trespass on your property or ride a horse that is known to throw its rider continually.

Every case is judged individually upon its merits and you will be best served by consulting a solicitor who has experience of equestrian matters.

Insurance
We have already seen how important adequate insurance is, but it will be useful to mention it again here in regard to any possible claims against you for damages.

Third party liability, or personal insurance, will cover you against possible claims arising from any damage your horse does to people or property, or from disease or accidental injury. So, when considering insurance, you should find a policy that will cover you against straying and accidental trespass, most likely where a horse gets loose from its field. All policies are subject to specific terms, conditions and exceptions, so if you are not sure of anything, ask the insurance company to explain it.

If you are only looking after or borrowing a horse, you should make sure that the horse's owner has the necessary insurance cover. This will ensure you are protected if the horse causes any damage or injury should it escape from your care.

As many older horses are kept solely at grass, it is worth mentioning here the influence the age of the horse has on insurance. Some companies will only insure up to a maximum age of 12, others go up to 15 or 16, while a few will insure a horse up to 20 years of age. However, look very carefully at the policy as what is actually covered might not be worth paying for.

Up to 12 years of age the insurers will cover vet's fees for injury and accident, or illness. However, once past 12 some policies only cover for injury and accident, not for illness, and some will limit the amount of cover per claim, so check this out if you have an older horse.

CHAPTER 4

THE STABLED HORSE

BUILDING A STABLE

When a horse is not kept in a livery yard, or at a friend's, most owners will want to have their horse at home if there is sufficient land. Unless you are planning to build a large complex, you should not have too much difficulty in obtaining outline planning permission to build a stable, and perhaps a tack room and feed store, from the local authorities. However, if you live in a conservation area, such as the National Parks, the Norfolk and Suffolk Broads, or in an area recognized as being of 'outstanding natural beauty', any building may be subject to certain limitations.

Before planning to build a stable you should check with your local council planning office that your land is not subject to an 'Article 4 Direction'. If it is you will need planning permission before going ahead. You should also check with them whether you will need approval under the Building Regulations, which means approval of your plans and materials. Any local by-laws relating to construction and/or drainage should also be checked.

Whether building a single stable or a new yard, you will benefit from the advice of a professional, who should save you time, money and many headaches!

SIZE AND DESIGN

Most horseowners will want to build a 'loose box' for their horse. This is what most people know as a 'stable'. A suitable size for a horse is 3.6 m (12 ft) by 3.6 m (12 ft), and for a pony 3.6 m (12 ft) by 3 m (10 ft), or 3 m (10 ft) by 3 m (10 ft) for a very small pony.

When designing a stable or stable yard the following basic needs of the horse need to be considered:

- a dry and warm area;
- adequate ventilation, ideally from a pure air supply;
- freedom from draughts and the prevailing wind;
- security, to prevent any unwanted people from entering unnoticed;
- good drainage, both in the stable and in areas where the horse may stand to be washed or hosed;
- good lighting, both natural and artificial;
- a suitable water supply.

SITE

While it may not be possible to site the stable in the ideal position, you should aim to put it where the ground is naturally drained; on gravel or

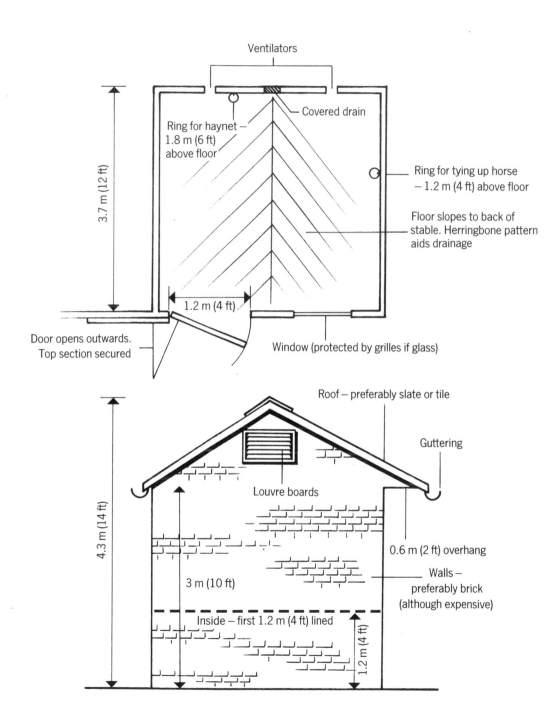

Ventilators

Covered drain

Ring for haynet –
1.8 m (6 ft)
above floor

3.7 m (12 ft)

Ring for tying up horse
– 1.2 m (4 ft) above floor

Floor slopes to back of
stable. Herringbone pattern
aids drainage

1.2 m (4 ft)

Door opens outwards.
Top section secured

Window (protected by grilles if glass)

Roof – preferably slate or tile

Guttering

Louvre boards

4.3 m (14 ft)

0.6 m (2 ft) overhang

Walls –
preferably brick
(although expensive)

3 m (10 ft)

Inside – first 1.2 m (4 ft) lined

1.2 m (4 ft)

A sample plan for a single loose box, which provides adequate ventilation and drainage.

chalk with a slight slope is ideal. If you are siting on clay soil you will need added drainage.

Make sure the doors and windows face south, to protect the horse from cold northerly or easterly winds. If this is not possible, then try to site the stable where a band of trees will act as a wind break.

It is important to site the stable where there is ease of access.

THE SAFE STABLE/ STABLE YARD

Floors should be roughened to provide a 'grip' when the horses are walking around or getting up from a snooze. Most people now use concrete as a base on which to erect a stable. It is easy to lay, can be made to have a rough surface and is easy to disinfect, so it is a good choice if mixed and laid well.

To allow adequate drainage stable floors should slope either forwards or backwards, but only slightly. The BHS recommends a fall of 1:48. Any wetness running from a concrete base should be directed to a drain outside the box, by a shallow gully.

When considering a design for the stable yard in relation to the safety aspects, much thought needs to be given to hay and straw storage, and the muck heap. Hay and straw can be stored in the same barn, although in separate stacks. To ensure stacks are not liable to topple over, you should employ a criss-cross design which will stabilize quite a tall stack. Plenty of air should be allowed to circulate between stacks, so corridors should be left between stacks.

The building which is used to house the hay and straw should be separate from the stable/s due to the risk of fire, and because many horses suffer from dust allergies.

An average horse will produce almost 3 tonnes of manure a year, so you need to consider where to put the

Safely stacked bales.

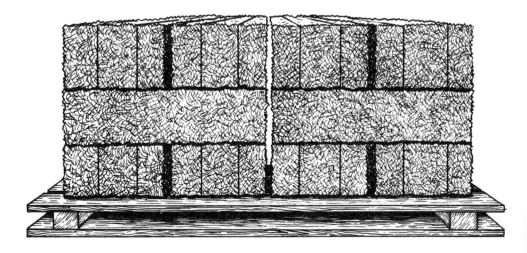

muck heap. It should be placed away from any stables and barns as a great deal of heat can be generated and, in very dry conditions, muck heaps have been known to burst into flames. There needs to be good access to the heap both by wheelbarrow, to aid the daily mucking out, and by tractor, to ensure it can be taken away. Horse manure is classed as domestic animal waste and you must, by law, ensure that the heap and resulting drainage do not cause:

ᴗ water pollution (by running into streams, for example);

ᴗ a nuisance to neighbours (by attracting flies into their garden or causing unacceptable smells), so it should not be positioned near a neighbour's boundary;

ᴗ a nuisance to someone else (for example, if the muck was removed from your premises and dumped on someone else's land).

Disposal of your muck heap is not as easy as you might think either. Under the Control of Pollution (Amendment) Act 1989, anyone disposing of your muck heap must be a registered waste carrier.

Stable fittings

Light switches are a common hazard. You should install approved watertight safety switches, if your stable does not already have them. These should be sited outside the stable, where the horse cannot reach over and chew them. Light bulbs must be protected in case your horse decides to try and eat them! A bulkhead fitting will give a good source of light inside a stable.

Exterior power outlets should have safety covers.

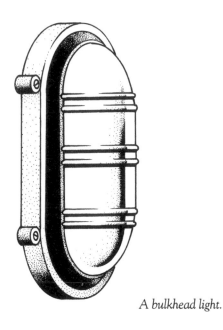

A bulkhead light.

An external power socket with cover.

Fittings used for feeding or watering should be kept to a minimum, as they only clutter up the stable and make it less safe. A manger should be of the removable corner type or one that fits over the door, so it can be taken down for cleaning. A corner manger should be fitted in the front corner of a stable, to prevent the horse having its hind legs towards you when entering or leaving the stable.

Horses who constantly knock their water over are a nuisance, so it may be necessary to use a wall bracket to hold the bucket. This should be hinged to fold flat when the bucket is taken out. Alternatively the water bucket could be put into an old tyre. Automatic watering bowls are suitable for horses, but they need to be kept free from hay or food.

Sample layout of stable fittings.

Putting a water bucket inside a tyre is a safe way of preventing the horse from knocking its water over.

Haynets should be tied up high enough so that the horse cannot get its foot caught in the holes. Hayracks are safe, but are less desirable to feed

hay from as little bits of hay may fall into the horse's eyes. Many people simply feed hay off the floor in the corner. This is safe of course, but can also be rather wasteful.

Salt lick holders are safe as long as they contain a new salt lick, but once the horse licks them down the edges protrude and provide the horse with something to catch itself on. It is far safer to put up an extra tie ring and tie a salt lick (of the variety with a hole in the middle) on to this.

Stable tools

Tools should be put in a safe place, away from horses and children. An area for tools should be designated, where all items are returned after use and properly put up. Forks or rakes lying about on the floor are simply waiting for someone to tread on or trip over them.

Doors and windows

Stable doors should be wide and high enough to allow a horse to pass through without injuring itself. A horse that rushes in or out of its stable is indicating that it is wary of banging itself because the opening is too narrow or too low.

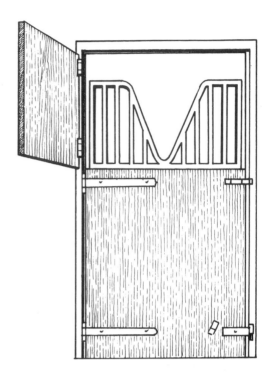

A conventional stable door with anti-weaving grille fitted.

Stable doors should be of the following minimum proportions:	
Width	1.1 m (3 ft 7 in)
Height of doorway	2.1 m (6 ft 10 in)
Height of lower door	1.27 m (4 ft 2 in)

Doors should also open outwards so that the horse's bedding does not prevent entry, especially in an emergency. Two bolts should secure the lower door. If the horse undoes the top one the bottom bolt will prevent it from escaping. Lower kick bolts (operated by the foot) stop you having to bend down to open the door and so save time in an emergency.

Windows should have a top vent that opens inwards and upwards to provide ventilation, but prevent draughts. The window should be covered with galvanized mesh for safety or protected by iron bars.

Electricity

As most stable fires are started through electrical faults, this is one

A good design for stable windows which will provide plenty of fresh air.

area that needs great consideration. All electrical installations should only be carried out by an approved contractor, who will ensure your requirements comply with present regulations. Any newly installed cabling should be well out of reach of any horse. It should also be waterproof, of a type which uses galvanized steel conduit or mineral insulated cable (MICV) with a PVC covering.

When choosing a site for the master switch panel, meters, trip switches and transformers, you should try to find a place out of the reach of horses and away from the weather. A separate tack room or shed would be ideal.

Any electrical appliances should also be checked regularly, including kettles and radios, as well as clippers or electric groomers.

Existing electricity cables and equipment should be regularly checked for signs of wear. Common problems to look for include the following:

U loose plug wires, where you can often see individual wires sticking out, rather than the usual thick PVC covering;

U wires chewed by mice or rats;

U wires cracked due to old age;

U split plugs and sockets;

U signs of overheating (discoloration) on plugs and sockets.

Horses are very susceptible to electrocution. In fact, it can be fatal. All stable yard circuits should therefore have a lifesaving residual current device (RCD) permanently wired into the circuit at the fuse box. An RCD is normally rated to operate at 30 mA (30 thousandths of an amp), and in less than half a second it will break the circuit and switch everything off if there is a fault anywhere in the wiring.

Fire prevention

Fire is one of the most important considerations, whether you have only one stable or a large stable yard. As many yard fires are started through electrical faults these areas need the greatest consideration.

Any faulty wiring should be immediately replaced and in any event it is a sensible precaution to have a qualified electrician carry out a maintenance check annually.

Other fires may be caused by carelessness when discarding cigarettes or matches, so every stable yard should enforce a no smoking policy and post No Smoking messages in prominent places.

There are many other measures you can take to make fire prevention a top priority.

To start with, you can install an alarm system, with smoke detectors in barns and stables. You should also have a fire point, housing fire extinguishers, a long hose-pipe which will reach all buildings, buckets of sand and empty buckets for water. Extinguishers should carry the BSI Kitemark BS5423 (for portable fire extinguishers) and BS6165 (for small, low-powered aerosol ones). Your local fire prevention officer, who can be contacted through your local fire station, will be only too pleased to offer help and advice. He will also

46

The fire point: every yard should have one.

advise on which extinguishers should be used for which types of fire: for example, liquid types should not be used on electrical fires. Remember to post a notice at the fire point stating where the nearest telephone is to be found.

You should also ensure that there are ample exits for the number of horses you keep and that the exits are kept clear at all times.

Leave headcollars near the stable/s so that in the event of a fire you can lead the horses out safely. Finally you should design a fire drill and practise it regularly.

47

Dealing with a stable fire

Being alerted to a stable fire is a frightening experience and happening upon one unawares is worse. However, you must keep calm and implement a plan of action, if a fire drill has not been previously established. First, of course, you must dial 999 to call the fire brigade. You will be asked your name and address, and the location of the fire.

If you are able, you should first release the horses that are closest to the fire. Put them into the nearest field or at least have them led away to the nearest safe place if there are helpers at hand. Even though other horses may not appear to be in danger, you should also remove them from the stables, since as once fire gets hold it spreads rapidly. If you can get at their headcollars, turn them out with these on. If not you will have to use belts or ties to lead them, remembering that they will be very anxious and their actions may be unpredictable.

Do not attempt to fight the fire until all the horses are safe, and then only if it is not dangerous for you to do so. If the fire is confined to a single stable or room, close all doors and windows (if possible, and without risk to yourself) to contain it. If the fire is slight and the horses are safe, you could try to put it out with the yard's fire extinguishers, hose or sand buckets. This is normally only possible if you actually see the fire starting and would be extremely dangerous if the fire was at all established. A fire extinguisher may prevent a small fire from becoming an inferno, but the fire brigade should always be called as well.

LAWS AND LIABILITIES

The provisions of the Health and Safety Act 1974 compel the staff of any establishment to understand the correct procedures in the event of *a fire*. If staff are aware of these and carry them through calmly they are likely to be able to save the lives of horses and/or the destruction of the yard should there be a fire. All staff should know where to locate fire-fighting equipment and how to use it. They should also know where to put the horses for their safety.

Apart from fire, you also need to be careful about the possibilities of stabled horses straying and catching infectious diseases.

To prevent *straying* from a stable, as opposed to a field (already discussed in Chapter 3), you need to ensure your horse's stable is secure. This involves making sure top and bottom bolts are fastened every time the door is closed. If your horse is known to be an escape artist, it is your responsibility to find a way of preventing it from releasing itself.

Many people use lead rope clips on the top bolts, to prevent the horse from raising the bolt to slide it back. However, such clips can be extremely dangerous and have been known to split a horse's lip open. There are some effective safety security bolts on the market, designed to prevent the cleverest escape-artist horse from either escaping or injuring itself on clips or bolts.

Infectious diseases are bad news, not only for the horse who is suffering, but for its owners as well.

If you are aware that your horse has a fungal skin ailment like ringworm, which can be passed on to both horses and humans alike, or a disease which is restricted to other equines, like strangles, you should be very cautious about allowing other animals or humans to come into contact with you while your horse is infectious.

You have a duty to inform others who are likely to come across your horse that it has an infectious disease and, of course, it should be isolated. You should not put the horse into a livery yard without informing the proprietor of its condition. The proprietor may ask you to keep the horse away until it has passed the incubation period or may make arrangements to have the horse totally isolated for this period.

You should not sell a horse with a warranty stating that it is free from infection. To your knowledge it may no longer be infectious – but it is possible that it is still infectious or has contracted some other disease.

In the case of a deceased horse, never get anyone to remove it without informing them of its infectious state. Diseases can still infect others after the horse has died. Similarly, you should never hide from a potential purchaser that a horse has an infectious disease or sell it at auction, where it will be able to pass on the condition.

If it were to be discovered that you had done any of these things you could be sued for damages.

INSURANCE

When taking out insurance you should inform your insurers where your horse is to be kept and whether it is to be stabled or kept at grass. Stabled horses may attract a lower premium as they are deemed to be more secure and at less risk of injury. However, if, having informed your insurers that you stable your horse every night, you then decide to keep it at grass, you should make this known to them.

You should also inform your insurers if your horse is injured or ill and needs attending by a vet, whatever the problem.

If your horse dies, or you claim for loss of use, further to an injury or illness contracted some time ago you can expect problems from your insurers, because of your late notification.

You are also expected to take all reasonable precautions to keep your horse in good health, including having it regularly vaccinated. If your horse gets tetanus from a cut because you failed to keep up with its vaccination boosters, your insurers may refuse to pay out.

Many horse policies also include stabling insurance. In the event that your horse's stable is totally destroyed by fire you will receive a set fee per week to stable it somewhere else, until a new stable can be rebuilt.

CHAPTER 5

TACK AND TURNOUT

Riding is both an expensive and a potentially dangerous sport, so when buying equipment it pays to ensure you get the highest quality and the safest standards for your money. The most expensive piece of equipment is not necessarily the best, however, so you need to know what you are looking for.

BUYING TACK

When buying items of tack remember that 'It's quality that counts'. A second-hand but good-quality piece of tack is always better than an inferior new one. High quality costs money, so having paid out for an expensive item, a previous owner is more likely to have maintained it well.

You should always buy from a reputable saddler, one that displays the Society of Master Saddlers' crest prominently at their premises. New and used tack can also be purchased from sales and auctions, but beware that they are ideal outlets for other people's cast-offs and inferior quality foreign items. Although it *is* possible to pick up the occasional bargain, if you know what to look for and, just as importantly, what not to look for, it is unwise to buy in this way as items may be defective and there are no guarantees to quality or suitability. In other words you are stuck with what

you buy and you might be compromising your horse's and your own safety.

UPKEEP OF EQUIPMENT

Good-quality tack is an investment that needs protection, and proper cleaning and maintenance are vital for your comfort and safety. Accidents occur when equipment breaks down as a result of neglect or poor-quality workmanship. There is little you can do about an item which has been made with an inherent fault, unless you discover it at the time of purchase or subsequently, when you should return it or discard it if you cannot return it. Defective tack should never be used as it is an accident waiting to happen.

Accidents due to neglect, however, are preventable. All tack and equipment should be wiped over after every ride, and cleaned thoroughly once a week. At this weekly clean any developing faults can be picked up and seen to before they become a safety risk.

Soaping leather items with a saddle soap containing glycerine will prevent leather tack from becoming dry and brittle, and will not rot the stitching. Using a suitable leather food from time to time will also help keep equipment soft and supple.

Leather should never be immersed in water or subjected to heat, such as being put into an airing cupboard after being drenched in the rain, or it will become brittle and may snap.

Hanging tack up correctly, with bridles on proper wall-mounted brackets, and saddles on saddle racks, will prevent damage due to carelessness. Saddles left on the backs of chairs or over the stable door can easily get knocked on to the floor and be damaged. If this does happen you should have your saddle checked by your saddler before using it again.

Bridles that are left on the floor or on chairs can easily be chewed by mice, or they can be tripped over by horses or people.

Checking for weak areas in tack/ equipment

While buying from a saddler who is a member of the Society of Master Saddlers will lessen your chances of obtaining a defective piece of tack, whether new or second-hand, inferior items do occasionally slip through unnoticed. It is therefore your responsibility to check your purchases for poor workmanship or faults.

It is also a sensible precaution to check your tack and equipment regularly so potential faults can be spotted. Quality tack, when cared for properly, should last a lifetime, although a certain amount of maintenance will be required from time to time.

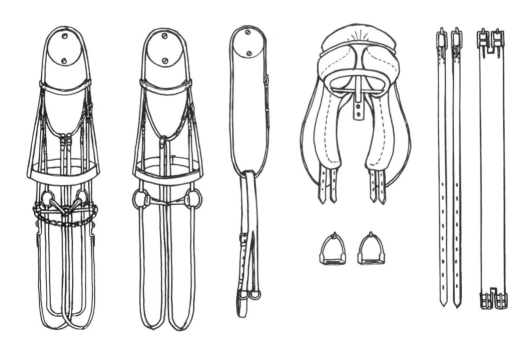

Tack put up safely.

When considering the condition of your tack look for the following.

U *Faults with the girth straps* Is the stitching securing the straps to the webs weak or perished? Are the holes in the straps stretched or split?

U *Weakness in the stirrup bar* Does the safety catch move freely or has it rusted in the 'up' position? Are the rivets still tight?

U *Weakness in any buckles or hook-stud fastenings* Are they corroded? Do they have sharp edges? Does the buckle tongue move freely – is it bent or loose? Is the hook stud bent or loose?

U *Loose or rotten stitching* Is it coming undone or has it rotted away altogether?

U *Sharp or loose bit rings and mouthpieces.*

○ *Cracked stirrup leathers, especially where they bend and pass through the stirrup iron* Stirrup leathers receive a lot of pressure so the stitching should be regularly checked.

○ *Cracked or split reins* Are the curves where the reins fix to the bit still in good order? Is the stitching secure? Reins also take a lot of pressure, so they should be given strict attention.

○ *Type of metal used in stirrup irons* Are they made of stainless steel, which is safe, or nickel, which can bend and break?

SAFETY WHEN TACKING UP

To prevent the horse from smashing you in the face while putting on its bridle or treading on your toes while saddling up, there are correct tacking-up procedures to follow.

Common weak areas of tack.

Putting on the bridle

1. Rest the rein buckle on the headpiece and hang the bridle over your left shoulder.

2. Stand on your horse's near side, take hold of its headcollar and unclip the lead rope.

3. Place the reins over its head and hold together under its neck, while removing the headcollar. Hang the headcollar up after removing it, otherwise you or your horse may trip up on it.

4. Hold the bridle in your left hand, put your right arm under your horse's jaw and around its head on the right side, resting your hand mid-way up its face.

5. Take hold of the bridle cheekpiece in your right hand, while still resting it on your horse's face, to prevent it from lifting its head.

6. Use your left thumb to encourage the horse to open its mouth and guide in the bit while drawing the bridle up its forehead. Ensure you keep your hand resting on its face to discourage your horse from raising its head.

7. Once the bit has been accepted, use your left hand to help pull the bridle gently over the horse's ears.

8. Do up the noseband and throat lash.

Opposite: Check all stitching before buying any tack and at every cleaning session. Any loose stitching should be seen to immediately.

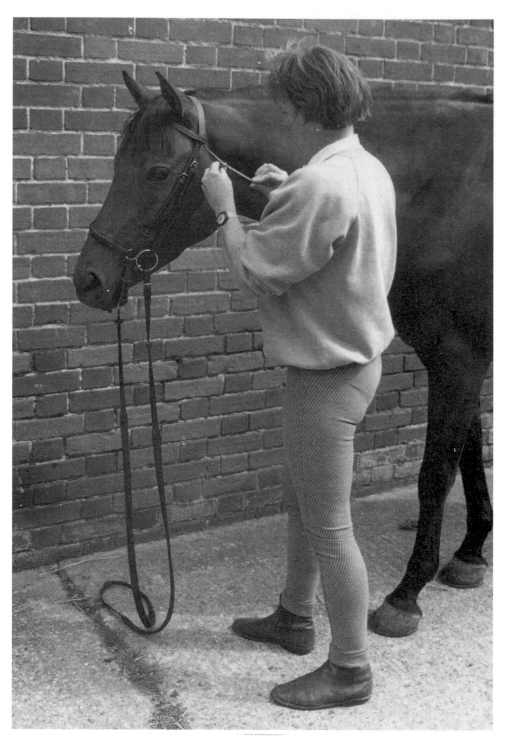

These reins are a safety hazard. The horse or handler could easily catch their feet in them and trip up, hurting the horse's mouth at the same time.

Putting on the saddle

1. Make sure the area underneath the saddle is clean.

2. Rest the girth over the saddle so that the buckles are facing you.

3. Gently place the saddle forward of your horse's withers and slide back into place until it comes to 'rest'.

4. Lower the girth on the offside, making sure the buckles do not hit the horse's offside leg.

5. Gently bring the girth under the horse's tummy, through the martingale loop if one is being used, and secure loosely on to the nearside girth straps.

6. Do up one hole at a time until the saddle is fastened securely.

7. Check the girth once again before mounting, and again after mounting, as many horses blow out when first saddled.

CORRECT FITTING

The correct fitting of a saddle is of paramount importance to your horse's comfort and your own safety. An ill-fitting saddle will cause the horse to rebel against the discomfort. The horse is likely to try and get rid of the pain, and this means you as well if you happen to be in the saddle at the time. Bridles, although they are easier to fit than saddles, can also cause problems if they are ill-fitting

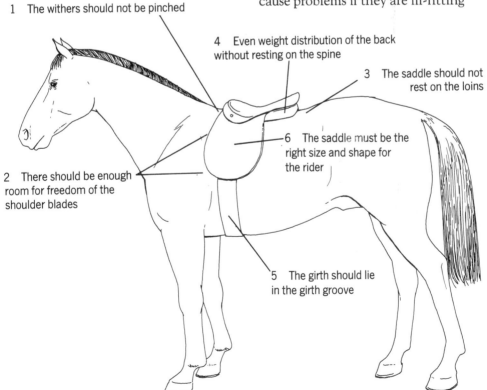

1 The withers should not be pinched

4 Even weight distribution of the back without resting on the spine

3 The saddle should not rest on the loins

6 The saddle must be the right size and shape for the rider

2 There should be enough room for freedom of the shoulder blades

5 The girth should lie in the girth groove

Correct saddle fitting

and no horse should be subjected to such treatment. It is an owner's or rider's responsibility to ensure all tack fits each horse properly.

When acquiring a saddle for your horse, whether new or second-hand, you should ensure it has been built on a BSI standard tree and that the tree is not broken or twisted. New British trees will bear the number BS6635 together with a letter for width fitting: W for wide; M for medium; and N for narrow. This number can be located on the stirrup bar. Have any saddle you intend to buy fitted and checked before purchase by a reputable saddler. It needs to fit your horse well and it also needs to fit you, the rider. Having obtained a well-fitting saddle you might find that after a few weeks' riding it becomes less than a perfect fit. This is because the flocking will have settled itself to the shape of your horse and to the rider's weight. The saddler will therefore often suggest a second visit to 'set up' the saddle again.

The bridle also needs adjustment once put on to ensure optimum comfort. You should be able to place a hand's width between the throat lash and the horse's face; and two fingers between a cavesson noseband (one between a drop, flash or grakle) and the horse's nose. The browband should fit snugly, but not pull the headpiece too tightly into the base of the horse's ears. The bit should fit snugly and allow a fingertip to be placed between the horse's lips and the bit rings. A jointed bit should slightly wrinkle the horse's lips, whereas a straight bar should fit up to the corners of the lips, but not wrinkle them.

SAFE RIDING CLOTHES

A hard hat is without a doubt the most essential piece of any rider's kit. Under section 218 of the *Highway Code*, children under 14 must, as a legal requirement, wear an approved safety helmet and fasten it securely. (Note: rules 216–24 and Road Traffic Law, section F of the *Highway Code*, deal with horseriders.) When selecting a riding hat you should ensure it has an approved level of protection. Such hats carry a BSI Kitemark; BS6473 for a riding hat and BS4472 for a jockey skull cap. These numbers are found inside the

A riding hat to BS6473 standard.

A jockey's skull cap to BS4472 standard.

When buying new items look for the BSI Kitemark.

hat. They also have a three or four-point harness which is much safer than the old two-point chin strap.

When using a riding hat you should make sure the drawstring inside the hat, if fitted, is done up properly. This will then provide a cushion of protection if you receive a blow to your head. You should ensure your hat feels comfortable and is fastened before mounting. It is also a good idea always to wear a hat when dealing with youngsters, or when lungeing or working a horse in-hand, and this is mandatory for service personnel.

SAFETY STIRRUPS

Science has recently been playing a large part in the design of equestrian safety equipment, yet there have been some good ideas about for many years.

Perhaps the biggest worry of many riders is falling off and being dragged. Because of this, various designs of stirrup have been manufactured to

For everyday safe riding you should wear the following.

- ∪ A BSI standard hat which has not previously received a significant impact (if it has it must be changed and destroyed.)

- ∪ A pair of gloves to prevent chafing from rubber reins and to prevent leather reins from slipping through your hands in wet weather. Gloves also help to keep your hands warm in cold weather, and this will ensure you can keep hold of the reins properly.

- ∪ Boots, whether long or short, with a suitable heel and protective toe caps.

- ∪ Comfortable clothes which will protect your arms, shoulders and legs in the event of a fall, and from low branches.

- ∪ Have your hair tied up, or wear a hairnet if it is long, to keep it from blowing into your face.

prevent the foot from either becoming trapped in or slipping through the stirrup.

The usual stirrup pattern is known as the *English hunting iron*. These stirrups should be the right size for the rider's foot, allowing about 1 cm (⅜ in) each side of the foot. As long as the rider is wearing a boot with an adequate heel and the stirrup is not too small or large for the rider's foot, there is very little chance of being dragged. Even in the unlikely event that your foot did somehow become jammed in the stirrup, your weight should easily pull the stirrup leather from its bar, providing the small safety catch is down. This safety catch should never be up.

For lightweight riders or children who might not be heavy enough to pull the stirrup leather from the saddle in this way, *Peacock safety stirrups* can be used. They have a thick, rolled rubber band attached outside of the iron, so that in the event of a fall the rider's foot will easily be released from the stirrup as the band simply pulls off.

Kournakoff stirrup irons.

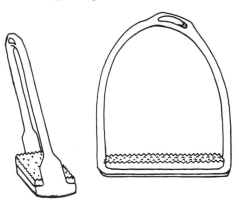

Correctly turned out for everyday riding.

Kournakoff stirrup irons are another type designed with safety in mind. They have an offset eye to the inside. The bars of the stirrup slope forwards, and the tread slopes upwards to encourage the toe to be higher than the heel, thus encouraging the foot to slip out of, rather than through, the stirrup.

Australian *Simplex* or *'bent leg'* *stirrups* have bulging forward bars on the outside. The idea is that if there is a fall the foot cannot become trapped.

Bent top stirrups have a 'bend' at the top. They should be fitted so they slope forwards, and are especially useful for those who have a tendency to push their foot well forward into the stirrup. They are also excellent when hunting as they do not rub the boot.

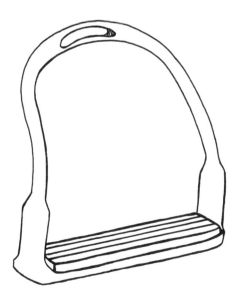

Bent top stirrup irons.

Whatever design is chosen, stirrups should always be used with treads. It is extremely dangerous to ride without them as they provide a non-slip surface for the foot to rest upon.

MATERIALS USED FOR TACK

Leather has always been the traditional saddlery material. However, synthetic tack is becoming increasingly more popular. It is hard-wearing, lightweight and totally washable. Both saddles and bridles are now manufactured in synthetic material, and are a boon to the busy owner/rider who does not have time for proper tack cleaning. They are also very good for use in the rain as they won't dry out and become brittle like leather if they do not receive time-consuming aftercare.

LAWS, LIABILITIES AND INSURANCE

If you buy tack from a saddlery retailer you will be covered by the Sale of Goods Act should an item prove faulty (or not 'fit for the purpose'). However, if you buy from a saddlery sale or auction you do not have the same protection under consumer law. So again – let the buyer beware!

Insuring your tack is also a sensible precaution and most policies cover it for fire damage, accidental damage or theft (following forcible/violent entry to a locked private building) on the same policy as your horse.

CHAPTER 6

LESSONS

LEARNING TO RIDE

In most cases learning to ride is a fairly straightforward process. You go along to an approved riding school, meet your instructor, get on the horse and learn how to ride. It is impossible to predict how long it will take before you are a competent rider, as everyone has different abilities. None the less the experience should be an enjoyable one.

Indeed, you can carry on quite happily until one day you fall off and break your arm – when you begin to look for someone to blame. This brings us back to the point made at the beginning of the book, that riding is a risk sport, and when you mount a horse you take that risk.

However, if you have taken the sensible step of going to an approved riding school, which is one approved by the BHS or the Association of British Riding Schools (ABRS) in the UK, you should be afforded some protection. Such schools are inspected periodically and can stay on the 'approved' list only if they come up to standard. This not only includes the standard of riding lessons given, but the quality of care and upkeep of the horses also.

Proprietors of riding schools must be very careful to ensure:

◡ that horses are matched to the ability of their riders;

◡ that all tack fits correctly, is in good repair and fit for its purpose;

◡ that all lessons or hacks are properly supervised, with a ratio of supervisors to riders reflecting the standard of riders in any particular lesson or ride.

Any proprietor who does not adhere to these 'rules' can be found negligent for not taking all reasonable precautions if there is an accident. (See Laws, liabilities and insurance, page 66.) Fortunately, however, accidents seldom occur, or if one does the rider is not usually too badly hurt and simply shakes him- or herself down and jumps back on.

CHOOSING A RIDING SCHOOL

You should never be put off learning to ride through fear of falling off, but you do need to find a riding school that will suit your needs. You may be looking for excellent facilities, such as an indoor school and cross-country course, while others will be happier with a smaller, more personal place.

It is always helpful to have a personal recommendation from a friend, especially if your friend does the same kind of riding as you want to do. However, if your friend has a really competitive nature, and rides at a school that teaches many competition riders, you may feel a little daunted by the place if all you want to do is learn to ride well enough to go for hacks.

Without a suitable recommendation you should buy a copy of the latest edition of the *BHS Where to Ride* booklet and/or the *ABRS Handbook*. These list hundreds of approved centres and at least one is bound to be fairly close to you. Having selected a few which seem to fit your needs, make a few telephone enquiries. You should ask these questions.

↺ *What facilities does the school have?* Do these match your requirements?

↺ *What will lessons/hacks cost?* Does this fit your budget? However, bear in mind that cheaper lessons may not benefit you in the long run. A more expensive private lesson might progress your ability twice as quickly as a less expensive class lesson.

↺ *How many horses/ponies does the school have?* Would you prefer to ride out on small hacks with only a couple of other riders or would you prefer a school with more 'hustle and bustle'?

↺ *How well schooled are the horses/ ponies?* Do you want to hack out on a nice, safe horse or do you want to get to Wembley?

↺ *How many instructors are there and what are their qualifications?* If you are a novice rider you might be happy with a younger, less qualified person, whereas if you are already riding at a fairly advanced level you will want a more qualified instructor.

Having asked your questions you will probably have whittled your list down to one or two schools that you would like to visit. While many establishments might fulfil your needs, you may have got an initial impression over the telephone that you did not like. Perhaps the person was not very helpful or they kept trying to get you to book a course of lessons over the telephone. Although we all have off days, first impressions do count.

Make an appointment to see the riding schools and instructors. On arrival take a good look around the yard. Is it clean and tidy? Do the horses look happy and healthy? Are the staff helpful and friendly? Look for the yard tools; are they put up safely? Are the riders wearing proper clothes and hats? If you like what you see ask if you may watch a lesson given by the instructor who is to teach you. Ask to meet the instructor and, if possible, discuss your requirements. Ask if you may book for an initial assessment lesson.

While all the above considerations are extremely important, as choosing the wrong riding school can be an expensive and possibly dangerous mistake, do be careful not to over- estimate your own ability. If you tell the instructor you have done some riding and are fairly good, you will come down with a bump if, after your assessment lesson, you are told you need to start from scratch. If, on the other hand, you are truthful and say you are a little anxious, your confidence will be given an enormous boost when your instructor tells you how well you have done in your first lesson!

INSTRUCTORS

The most important step towards learning to ride will be finding the right instructor. You will instantly know whether you are likely to hit it off and, if you are at all doubtful about your compatibility, you should think twice before going ahead with any lessons.

Success in learning to ride, whether as a beginner or as a more advanced student, will depend upon three factors: your instructor; the horse you ride; and yourself. This can effectively be called the 'triangle of learning'. You need to respond well to your instructor; your horse needs to respond well to you; and your instructor needs to evaluate the

feedback he or she gets from both of you and devise a lesson plan accordingly.

The instruction you receive should depend upon your ability and most riding schools will try to match you with an appropriate instructor. The BHS has four standards of instruction: the Preliminary Instructor; the Intermediate

Instructor; the Instructor; and the BHS Fellow.

The ABRS has one standard: the ABRS Teaching Certificate. The holder of this certificate must show an ability and willingness to teach the all-important weekly rider.

YOUR RIGHTS AS A PUPIL

Hopefully, your riding lessons will all go according to plan and you will be happy with the level of instruction you receive. How well you progress will depend upon you as an individual and on the regularity of your lessons. What happens, then, if you are less than pleased with the service you are receiving?

You can either complain to the proprietor or move schools. Many people do not like to complain, as they feel their lessons will suffer further with their instructor prejudiced against them, and in any event the atmosphere which is likely to result will not be conducive to learning. Also, it may not be convenient to change schools. So what should you do?

First, you should ensure you are not expecting the impossible and then try to discuss the matter diplomatically with your instructor, explaining where you feel things are going wrong. As a guide it is fair to expect your instructor to want to get to know you and treat you as an individual, not a 'novice number'; and to be reliable and, apart from illness or exceptional circumstances, always be

The condition of the yard will tell you a lot about an establishment.

there for your lesson. Changing instructors every lesson will not see a fair level of progression. Your instructor should be experienced and able to instil confidence in you, showing a mature attitude towards your lessons and respecting your wishes. An instructor should also be enthusiastic and make lessons fun and educational, and above all be cheerful, friendly, helpful and encouraging.

SAFETY AT THE RIDING SCHOOL

While you are at a riding school there are certain 'rules' which should be obeyed in the interests of safety. First, children should always be under supervision. They are apt to get excited when they see horses, and can shout and jump about. This may frighten the horses who, if they start to leap around as well, could cause an accident.

Secondly, you should only go into areas designated for the public. While many schools will not object to you watching the horses being groomed or tacked up, and some may even like you to help, you should ask first.

Finally, do not leave anything lying about where a horse or people may trip over it, or park your car where it may cause an obstruction.

Safe riding in groups

On many occasions you will find yourself riding, in an outdoor school (known as a manège) or in an indoor school, with other horses and riders. To prevent you all from running into each other, certain unwritten 'school rules' should be observed:

ʊ ask permission from anyone already in the school before entering;

ʊ always close the gate after you;

ʊ refrain from producing noisy distractions;

ʊ do not carry on a conversation with other riders, as this will interfere with both your and their concentration;

ʊ pass an approaching horse on the opposite rein, observing the rule of left hand to left hand, giving riders on the left rein priority;

ʊ avoid interrupting faster-moving horses;

ʊ leave a distance of at least 1.5 m (4ft 6in), between yourself and any horse in front;

ʊ be prepared to stop immediately and dismount in the event of an accident.

Apart from preventing accidents the discipline of following such rules has a beneficial effect, requiring you to concentrate on your riding skills and to remain alert at all times.

HEALTH AND SAFETY AT WORK

Working with horses is physically demanding and many tasks can lead to accidents if a safe method of work is not enforced. The Health and Safety at Work Act 1974 places general duties on employers to

When viewing a horse before purchase, ask to see it trotted up to make sure it is sound.

A horse with good conformation.

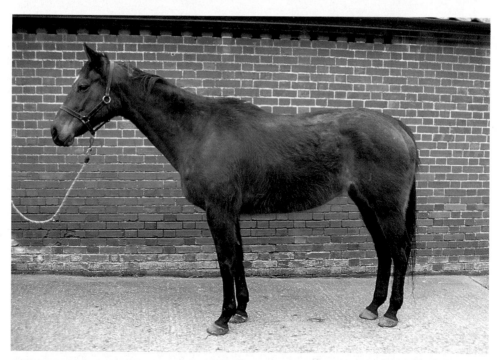

A horse with poor conformation, which is made worse by its poor condition. Do not be tempted to buy such a horse out of pity.

Above: Approach the horse from the
and slightly to the side.

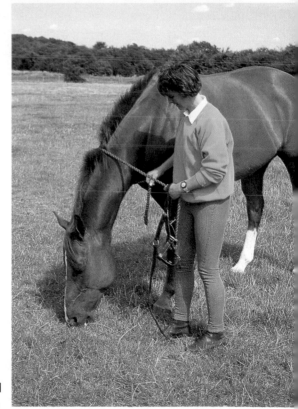

Right: Slip the lead rope around the
horse's neck, so that you have a hold
on it while putting on the headcollar.

Left: To prevent other horses from escaping, keep hold of the gate while walking the horse into the field.

Below: This grooming box is a safety hazard; either the handler or the horse could easily trip over it.

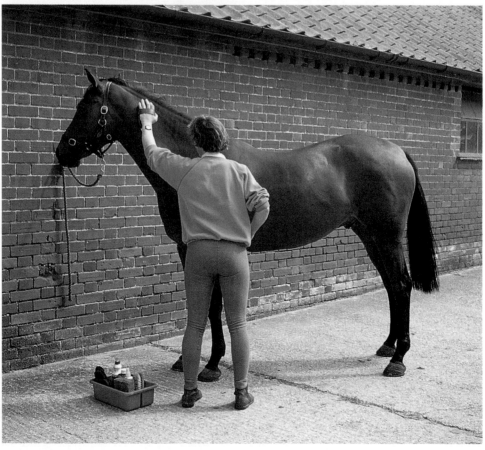

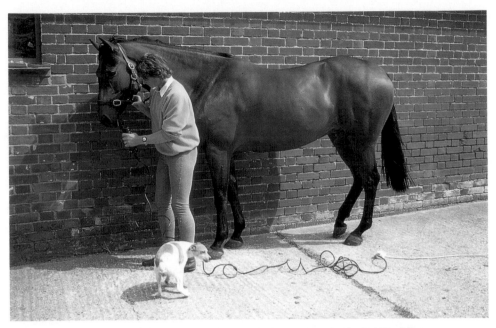

Dangerous: were the horse to move it could easily tread on the lead of these clippers and be electrocuted. The dog should also be locked away as it could cause the horse to jump about, and could get hurt itself.

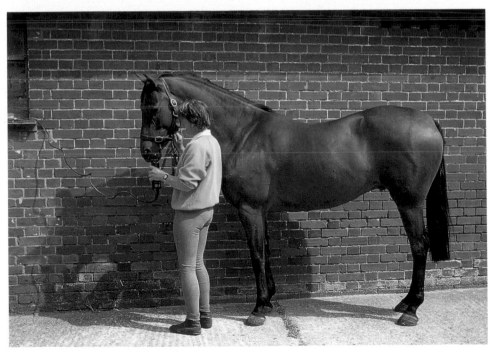

Safe: the lead is up out of the way and so is the dog!

Dangerous: throwing a rug over a horse's back like this could frighten it.

Safe: the rug is folded back into place, having been laid gently on the horse's back.

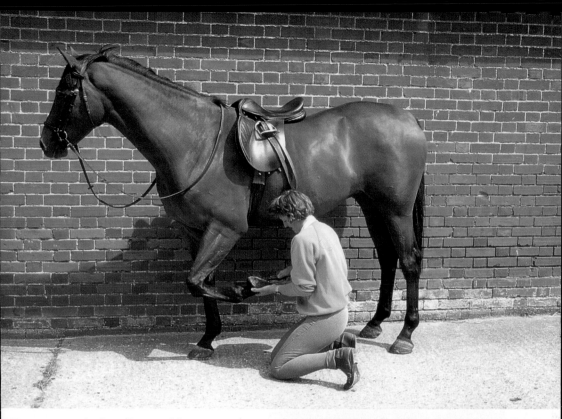

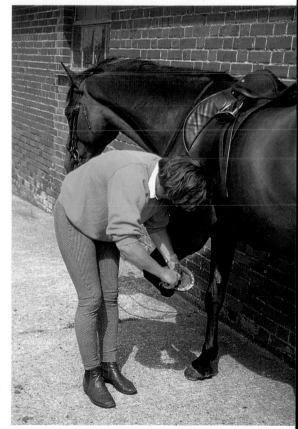

e: Dangerous: the handler would
no chance of moving away
ly, and could get jumped on.

Right: Safe: the handler can jump out of
the way quickly should this be
necessary.

Above: Regularly picking up droppings from the pasture will help to keep the worm count down.

Left: Ragwort. It is poisonous to horses and can cause great damage over a period of time.

Above: Check all new fields before turning a horse out as dangerous objects could be lurking in overgrown grass.

Right: Every horse must receive regular attention from the farrier. Do all that you can to keep a good farrier once you have found one.

Dangerous: leaving tools on the floor is lazy and could cause a nasty accident if someone trips over them.

Safe: stable tools put up neatly.

Dangerous: this pony could very easily put her foot through the haynet. It should be tied up much higher and on to a tie ring, not directly on to the fence.

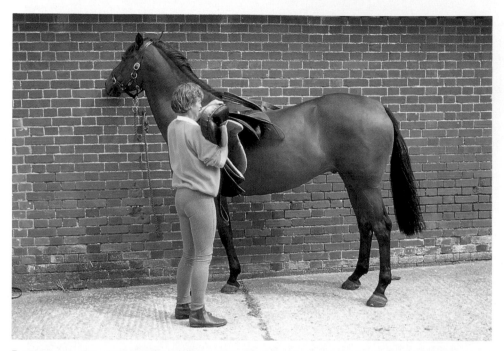

Dangerous: the girth has been placed on the horse's back first, and will slip down and bang against the horse's leg when the saddle is put on.

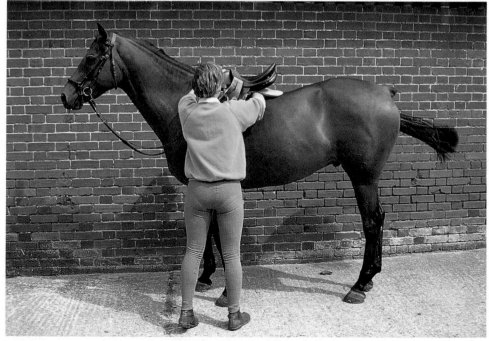

Safe: the girth is folded over the saddle before it is gently placed on the horse's back.

Above: Regular cleaning and maintenance will help keep tack in a safe condition.

Left: Ensuring the correct fit of a saddle.

Left: Every riding establishment should display a copy of their rules and fire drill in a prominent place.

Below: A safely conducted class lesson with plenty of room between horses.

Right: Hacking in the countryside can bring immense pleasure, and all riders should endeavour to follow the Countryside Code.

Below right: Be Safe Be Seen. Horse and rider correctly turned out for riding in the evening or early morning.

Above: When jumping you should give your horse and the course your full concentration.

Right: Marking tack with metal identity punches will help identify your equipment if it is recovered after a theft.

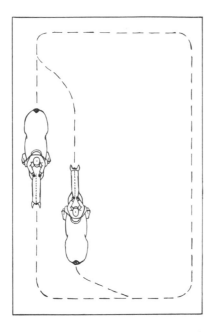

Safe riding in the school, observing the rule of 'left hand to left hand'.

Learning how to lift and carry things correctly will minimize the risk of injury.

ensure the health and safety of their employees. To comply with the Act an employer must provide safe methods of work; a safe and healthy workplace; and adequate training, instruction and supervision for the tasks undertaken by employees.

In 1986, extra requirements to the 1974 Act were published, so now anyone wanting to set up a yard should obtain the Horse Riding Establishment Guidance on Promoting Safe Working Conditions from the Health and Safety Executive. There are many general obligations covered in these rules, and these are all designed to ensure employees and third parties (in this case you, the riding pupil) are afforded the healthiest and safest conditions possible.

RECORDING INCIDENTS OR ACCIDENTS

It is compulsory for every BHS- or ABRS-approved school to keep an incident or accident book. The book should keep a record of the time, place and date of any incident or accident, and should have written in it a true account of what actually took place. While the details may seem trivial at the time they may be extremely important if a claim for damages is made later. The instructor at the time of the accident may have left the riding school, and witnesses may move, so the only sure account of what happened is what is recorded in the incident/accident book. Having made the appropriate notes, the person in charge at the time should sign to acknowledge that they are a true account of what happened, and so should the injured party and any witnesses. The name and address of any witness should also be recorded. (For dealing with accidents see page 74.)

THE RIDING ESTABLISHMENTS ACTS

A 'riding establishment' is defined as a business that keeps horses either for the purpose of their being let out on hire, or for the purpose of conducting riding lessons for payment, or both.

Thus, the Riding Establishments Acts 1964 and 1970 provide that riding schools can only be conducted under a licence which is granted by the local authority.

This is applicable in England, Scotland and Wales. A similar act entitled Riding Establishments Regulations 1980 applies in Northern Ireland and the Riding Establishment (Inspection) Act 1968 applies in the Isle of Man.

A local authority will only grant such a licence if it is sure certain minimum standards are being observed. Licences have to be renewed annually and checks are made to ensure required standards are being met.

The Riding Establishments Act 1970 states that the licence holder must hold a current public liability insurance policy to give indemnity against liability. This will cover accidents that happen to anyone hiring a horse or having lessons. It will also cover accidents that might happen as a result of the rider injuring another person while on the hired horse or during a lesson.

LAWS, LIABILITIES AND INSURANCE

All riding schools and training centres should be covered for negligence under their insurance policy and this will offer you cover if you get hurt due to their negligence. However, the policy will not cover an accident that was deemed to be plain bad luck.

If you inform the riding school that you are a beginner or require special instruction and they undertake to teach you to ride, or coach you in a certain discipline, they have entered into a contract with you. However, there are few people who would insist on having a written contract, and in any case it would be very difficult to lay down exact terms and conditions.

What the riding school should ensure, however, is that you are taught by a qualified instructor who has the necessary skills to teach novice riders or give special instruction, as appropriate. They should also ensure that the horse you are given to ride is fit and suitable for the purpose, and that the tack used on the horse is safe.

In the event that the instructor proves less than capable of teaching you, or the horse is highly strung and clearly not suitable for the purpose, or the bridle slips off the horse because it was far too big for it, and as a result you fall off, you would have a claim against the riding school for breach of an 'implied term' (a term legally held to be implied in your contract).

Any riding carried out from the riding school, whether in the school or out on the roads, needs proper supervision. For example, it is not sufficient to have one experienced escort take out a line of horses with novice riders on a hack, unless there are also other supervisors, both mounted and as leaders/unmounted helpers. If one such rider fell off while out on a hack that was not adequately supervised the proprietor could face a claim for negligence. If, however, the proprietor took all reasonable precautions and due to some unforeseen circumstance a rider fell off, the proprietor is unlikely to be held responsible.

In the interests of your own safety it is a good idea to think about insurance protection for yourself, especially if you borrow a horse or if you ride regularly but don't own your own horse. A few insurance companies offer rider-only cover or specially designed rider plans. While you can enhance your own personal safety by wearing the correct gear and being sensible while riding or attending horses, you can never know what might happen. Not all accidents can be prevented, so it pays to cover yourself. If you are working you should also look into the possibility of covering yourself against loss of earnings should you be injured.

CHAPTER 7

HACKING AND ROAD SAFETY

ROAD SAFETY IN PRACTICE

The BHS's research has shown that there are almost 3,000 accidents a year involving horses and vehicles on the roads. This is a horrifying statistic that responsible riders should aim to reduce by not adding their names to the list.

It is all too easy for riders to blame motorists for every accident that involves a horse; but instead of looking to apportion guilt, riders should take positive action now to reduce the toll.

What is needed is a mutual understanding and awareness between riders and motorists to ensure that the roads become safer for all who use them.

Riders need to act sensibly on the roads, being courteous to other road users and aware of their needs as well as riders' own.

Motorists need to recognize that horses are not 'vehicles', and are often unpredictable, especially if frightened in some way.

PREPARATION FOR RIDING ON THE ROADS

One of the first things you need to ask yourself before hacking out is 'Are my horse and I ready for the road?' You might already give a physical check to your tack, but do you give a mental check to your horse's behaviour and plan your route accordingly?

Having checked that your tack is in good repair and correctly fitted and that you have on safe riding wear, you should also consider the following.

℧ *The weather and time of day* Do you or your horse need reflective and/or fluorescent clothing and lights? (In accordance with *Highway Code* rule 219, a safety lamp, showing white light to the front and red to the rear, should be fitted on the offside stirrup after lighting-up time, as defined in the code.)

℧ *The sort of work you and your horse are going to be doing* Should you be wearing a back/body protector?

℧ *Whether you are properly insured* You can be held liable if your horse causes damage to other people or their property.

Correctly turned out for road riding.

↻ *Whether you have read and understood the Highway Code* The *Highway Code* does apply to horseriders, and when on the public highway you have the same rights and responsibilities as other road users.

↻ *Your horse* Is it young, nervous or traffic shy? If it is, do you have a friend with an older horse with whom you could ride? Can you plan your route to keep away from busy roads?

BHS RIDING AND ROAD SAFETY TEST

Everyone who uses the public highway, whether it be a busy main road or a country lane, is at risk. One

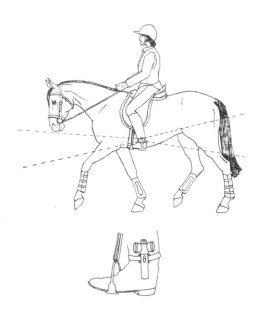

Stirrup lights showing white to the front and red to the rear.

positive thing everyone can do to reduce the risks involved in road riding is to take the BHS Riding and Road Safety Test, and be wise to the roads. Only when riders are fully visible to other road users will we be on level terms with them.

The test aims to give riders some form of recognition for acting responsibly, showing courtesy to other road users, and complying with the law and recommendations set out in the *Highway Code* and the *BHS Riding and Road Safety Manual*.

Once you have satisfied yourself that you and your horse are prepared for safe road riding, you can then consider what you need to know in order to take the test. Training sessions for the test may be available through your local BHS-approved centre, or through Pony Club rallies, which the local BHS road safety representative will attend.

By the time you have completed your training sessions, you should be able to show competence in a number of situations.

- ∪ *Signals* Because horses are not vehicles, you need to use signals that will not only 'inform' other road users of your actions, but which will also 'influence' the way in which they will behave towards you. You should learn how to inform other road users of your proposed actions, and so in your first few training sessions the instructor will describe and demonstrate signalling procedure, and how to give signals clearly and decisively.

- ∪ *Traffic lights and junctions* While it would be nice not to have to

negotiate such obstacles, in reality few people can get away without having to use them at some time or another. Therefore, knowing the correct procedure to follow when you encounter traffic lights or junctions is of great importance.

- ∪ *Passing and overtaking stationary vehicles* When passing stationary vehicles, you should also follow the correct procedure and think ahead. Is the person sitting in the vehicle suddenly going to open the door? Is something going to be unloaded from the back of that lorry as you pass? If practicable, you should give a verbal warning of your presence and request politely that you be allowed to pass without them making any sudden movements. Always be sure to acknowledge consideration shown by such actions. Also, oncoming traffic does have the right of way, so you need to stop and let it pass first before manoeuvring.

- ∪ *Hazards and dismounting* Similarly, when approaching hazards, think ahead and be prepared, anticipating your horse's reaction. The safest place to be is on your horse's back and you should endeavour to stay there unless it is absolutely essential to dismount. If you make the decision to dismount, do so as quickly and with as little fuss as possible.

- ∪ *Leading and remounting* If it is necessary to lead a horse on the road, perhaps because of lameness

The BHS Riding and Road Safety Test: here the rider correctly signals left as the lights turn to green.

or a hazard, you should do so correctly. Most people lead a horse from the nearside, but this is incorrect when leading on the roads. While you keep to the left of the road at all times, the idea is to put yourself between the horse and the traffic, and so lead from the offside – indeed, this is a *Highway Code* requirement. To remount it is sensible to try and find a gateway or wide verge where you can do so safely. Care should be taken not to allow the horse to swing its quarters out into the traffic. If you anticipate that your horse is likely to try and swing away from you when mounting, consider mounting from the offside to keep the horse square.

U *Defensive riding* There are times when it is sensible to ride defensively. For example, you might need to keep out from the kerb to make sure a motorist can see you and slow accordingly, before pulling back in to let them past. While you should not obstruct other road users unduly, you do have just as much right to be on the roads and should wait for a safe moment to pull into the side to let others pass.

To stay alert, be observant and ride defensively with anticipation is the essence of safe horsemanship.

Once you have completed your training sessions, where you will have covered roadcraft, the *Highway Code*, accident procedure and insurance cover, your instructor will be able to give you details on how and where you take your test.

The test itself

The test itself is divided into three parts. Part One: Theory is designed to test your knowledge of the *Highway Code*, and the meaning of traffic signs and signals. You will also be required to know the generally accepted rules for riding safely on the public highway as set out in the *BHS Riding and Road Safety Manual*. You might simply be asked questions or you may be given a multiple-choice test paper. In any event the examiner is looking for factual answers not opinions.

In Part Two: A Simulated Road Route a mock route is constructed with traffic lights, road junctions and hazards similar to normal road conditions. The examiner will be looking at what precautions you take against a series of sights and sounds that might reasonably be met on the road, and at which a horse might shy, and will assess your reactions to such situations.

Always remember the safety code for riding. You should:

U thank other road users who give way and show consideration;

U be considerate and try to help other road users;

U be observant and avoid difficult situations by thinking ahead;

U request permission from riders in front before passing them;

U pass other riders or pedestrians on bridleways or narrow paths at a walk;

U always look behind before making any manoeuvre.

In Part Three: Road Test on the Public Highway you will be tested in genuine road conditions. The examiner will want to be satisfied that you have a good understanding of roadcraft, and that your knowledge and application of the requirements of the *Highway Code* are sound.

OFF-ROAD RIDING

One of the greatest developments for safer riding has been the BHS's ARROW (Access and Riding Rights of Way) campaign to discover and open up all the UK's off-road tracks and paths. The aim is to achieve a countrywide network of riding routes without the risk of traffic in all counties of the UK.

Off-road riding can be classified into two categories: rights of way, such as bridleways or roads used as public paths (RUPPS); and riding by kind permission, on a farmer's land, for example.

Take the time to visit your local farmers and ask if they mind you riding around the edges of their fields or along paths made by their tractors. If they give their permission, and most will, ask if there is anywhere to avoid. They may allow shooting in their woods, for instance. If you are given permission remember to close gates and keep off growing crops – do not abuse their trust.

Rights of way are tracks and paths which you are entitled to use free of charge. Look at your local Ordnance Survey map to find your rights of way.

Always remember to close gates if you open them when out hacking.

You may be surprised to see that there are more bridleways than you thought, since not all are signposted as they should be.

Byways, although open to all, are often little used, except perhaps by the odd tractor. They are quite useful as they usually link one lane to another, often avoiding the more busy roads.

RUPPS, or 'greenlanes' as they are often called, are open to riders. However, they are also open to motorcyclists and other forms of vehicles, but there might be an 'unsuitable for motor vehicles' sign up.

When hacking out it is a good idea to go with a friend as you never know what you might come across on 'unknown' routes. If you have to ride alone always let someone know where you are going.

ACCIDENTS

We are all probably guilty of thinking 'It'll never happen to me', especially if we do not ride competitively, but approximately 65 per cent of all riding accidents happen while riding for pleasure.

Very few riders are fortunate enough to ride nowadays without having to negotiate busy roads; so the prospect of having a road accident is a constant worry.

Why do accidents occur?
In trying to prevent road accidents it is most important to consider why they occur. It will probably surprise you to learn that riders have as many opportunities to be as much at fault as the motorist.

U Some accidents happen because a rider is not wearing reflective gear in poor light or at dusk and the driver of the vehicle simply doesn't see them. Even if you are only leading a horse down the road to its field you should make sure that you and your horse are clearly visible.

U Some riders are silly enough to ride alone on the roads on a horse known to be unsafe in traffic.

U Sometimes a motorist is simply going too fast to be able to slow down in time and if the rider is unable to get out of the way the car hits the horse. Sadly, the horse usually comes off worst.

U Sometimes a driver does not slow down enough when seeing a horse playing up, resulting in horse and car colliding.

U Other accidents can occur when no cars are present. The horse may slip on ice, for example, or simply shy and unseat the rider. While such incidents seem frightening at the time, they rarely produce serious casualties, especially if the rider is wearing correct clothing and headgear.

U Occasionally riders have failed to check their tack before a ride and the stitching has given way, perhaps on the girth or reins. Obviously, the seriousness of the accident depends on how fast the horse is travelling at the time, but imagine suddenly feeling the saddle going from under you while galloping – or finding yourself with only one rein while trotting down the high street!

Accident prevention

Knowing why accidents occur can provide us with the information to help prevent them.

1. Be Safe Be Seen. Avoid riding at dusk, in poor weather such as heavy fog, or after dark if possible. If you *are* riding in such conditions ensure you and your horse wear reflective clothing, and use stirrup lights showing red to the rear and white to the front. Always carry reflective armbands and legbands in your pocket in case you get caught out.

2. Always ride with someone else, especially if your horse is not good in traffic or if riding a youngster.

3. Defensive riding: put positive thought first. Take up a position in the road where you can be clearly seen, or ride two abreast if in company, in order that motorists have to slow down before they can overtake. Hugging the kerb may induce fast and unsafe overtaking.

4. Being courteous to motorists informs them that slowing down and showing consideration to horses and riders is very much appreciated.

5. Always obey the *Highway Code* and act upon road signs and signals in the correct manner. Make use of verges and gateways where possible, and when appropriate.

6. Make sure your tack is safe every time you ride.

7. Be prepared to dismount and lead your horse if conditions become so dangerous that this is your only recourse.

8. Ensure both you and your horse are fit. Overtiredness increases the risk of injury.

9. Ensure you wear safe clothing and headgear. Knee protectors are also a sensible precaution for your horse.

10. No matter how well you know your horse, always be on your guard when out hacking. Horses are unpredictable – you should never become complacent.

Accident procedure

While you can cut down on the risks, you will not be able to eliminate accidents altogether and unfortunately they will occur from time to time. There is always the possibility that you may have to cope with a serious riding accident at some time, and dealing with such a situation competently could literally mean the difference between life and death for the injured rider.

Helping someone who has had an accident can be quite frightening, especially if you don't know what to do. Therefore, every rider should endeavour to learn the essential basics of first aid, including life-saving skills. The best way of doing this is to attend sessions held by the St John Ambulance group.

If it is the horse that has been injured call for veterinary assistance immediately. By dialling 999 you can inform the police, who will contact the nearest available vet for you.

While you can deal with the injuries in the same way as you would deal with a human's, there is little else you can do for the horse except keep it warm if possible and protect its head with your coat if it is on the floor. Even if the horse appears unhurt it will probably be suffering from shock.

At the scene of an accident

Whether or not you feel a motorist is to blame for any accident you should always make sure that the police have been notified of what has happened.

Any motorist contributing to an accident should stop but some don't, or drive off as soon as the way is clear for them to do so. It will pay you to practise memorizing vehicle registration numbers; in an accident it is vital for you to do so, and to remember the colour and make of the vehicle involved. Note the time of day as this may help in tracking down the motorist.

Even if the motorist does stop, take down his or her name and address as soon as you have administered any necessary first aid. They might volunteer to go for help – only to be never seen again.

If there were witnesses to the accident take down their names and addresses, and pass these on to the police.

Also write down any facts that you think might be relevant in case the driver is sued for damages on the grounds of his or her negligence. Note the weather at the time, the road conditions – either busy or quiet, for example – and the state of the road surface. As soon as you are able to, make a good sketch of the scene. Be sure to show the position of the vehicle accurately in relation to the horse. Even if you are the injured party, and you feel you or your horse are perhaps to blame, never admit liability. Simply exchange insurance details with the motorist and leave the insurance company to sort it out. Notify your own insurance company of what happened as soon as possible.

Finally, fill in the BHS traffic accident report form (S03) as such data provide the BHS with valuable statistics, helping them to press for safer roads and riding conditions.

Claims for damages arising from road accidents

If you are ever involved in a collision with a motor vehicle you could consider claiming damages for:

◡ physical injury;

◡ psychological injury;

◡ value of horse if fatally injured or reduction in the value of horse;

◡ cost of a temporary substitute horse;

◡ cost of locating a suitable replacement horse, including veterinary examination fees;

◡ cost of having the horse put down and of its removal;

◡ livery expenses during nursing and recovery;

◡ cost of replacing damaged saddlery;

◡ your loss of earnings.

While these might be the furthest things from your mind if your horse is hurt, there will come a time when you might find an award of damages useful.

LAWS, LIABILITIES AND INSURANCE

While an accident can happen when riding at home, you take more risks when riding on the roads, not only to your personal safety but to others as well, because you will be coming into contact with other road users, including pedestrians, and you may unknowingly stray on to private land.

As far as the law is concerned you will not be *automatically* held responsible if your horse strays on to private property, whether you are

riding it or not. You may be leading the horse home after it has lost a shoe, for instance.

The law says that a person owning property next to a public road should accept some of the risks and if their fencing is poor it may be taken into account.

You would be negligent, however, if while you left your horse alone, perhaps tied to a friend's drainpipe while you nipped in for a cup of tea, it got loose and caused damage on someone else's land.

In summary, you should take extra care while out hacking. You should never knowingly ride on private property without permission, even on verges in front of houses, or leave your horse unattended while out on a ride.

CHAPTER 8

IN COMPETITION

With an ever-increasing number of equestrian events, from the local gymkhana to an 80-km (50-mile) long distance ride, more and more riders are taking part in equestrian sports. When a large number of riders converge on a small space, safety risks are bound to be higher. Horses and riders get excited or become nervous, which can lead to a lapse of concentration.

However, if everything is prepared well in advance and you arrive at the show in plenty of time, there will be no need for panicking. On arrival at the venue you can take time to get yourself and your horse ready and should have a much more enjoyable day as a result.

While there is immense pressure on the top riders to try and win, you will have no such obligations to any owners or sponsors. Of course, you will wish to do well and anyone who denies that winning or being placed gives a real feeling of satisfaction is talking nonsense, but every true sportsperson remembers that it is the taking part which counts. If you only derive pleasure from winning, then perhaps you should think about giving up. Otherwise one day you may push yourself and your horse so hard that you ignore all the safety precautions and that is when accidents happen.

SAFETY WHEN TRAVELLING

Most people transport their horses to shows in horseboxes or trailers. Not only do they allow you to go to shows some distance away, but they also allow you to leave your horse tied up in relative safety, although there should always be someone supervising in case of an accident.

Any vehicle used to transport a horse should be in a roadworthy condition; that is, it should have good brakes, oil, water and enough fuel to get you there and back comfortably. You should check that everything is working before loading any horse into the vehicle, including lights and windscreen wipers. It also needs to be taxed and insured, or, in the case of a trailer, this will apply to the towing vehicle.

Your horse should be protected from injury during any journey. Protective clothing that should be used includes:

Ʊ travelling boots or bandages;

Ʊ a tail bandage or tail guard;

Ʊ knee caps and hock boots, if the travelling boots are not all in one;

Ʊ a poll guard;

Ʊ a rug, of the correct thickness to match the weather.

Before loading your horse into a vehicle ensure that it is both wide and high enough to allow it to stand in comfort.

Unless you are going to do strenuous work soon after unloading you should give your horse a haynet to pick at on the journey, as it will travel far more contentedly. If you are transporting only one horse in a double trailer, which has a centre partition, always load the horse on the right-hand side. If using the same trailer without a centre partition, tie the horse's head to both sides of the trailer to prevent it from attempting to turn around.

When loading your horse, bear the following in mind:

ʊ wear gloves;

ʊ do not wrap the lead rope around your hand;

ʊ do not stand in front and pull the horse;

ʊ walk in the centre of the ramp;

ʊ do not tie the horse until the partitions or breeching strap are in place;

ʊ tie it up on a short lead using a quick release knot.

A horse turned out safely for travelling.

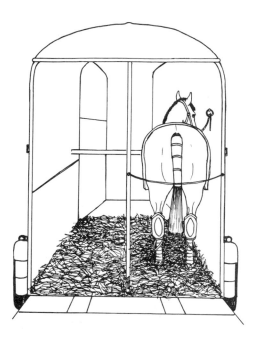

If only transporting one horse in a double trailer, always travel it on the right-hand side.

Always load your equipment and get everything ready before loading your horse. As soon as you have loaded your horse, you will then be able to drive straight off. Most horses object to being loaded and then standing still for ages, and some will show their annoyance by kicking back or trying to break free.

When unloading your horse on arrival you should untie it and ensure the breeching strap is still secure, before letting down the ramp. Having lowered the ramp your horse cannot then back out until you undo the breeching strap. When you do so you will then be able to gain control of it by taking hold of the lead rope and backing it steadily down the centre of the ramp.

The way you drive your horsebox or trailer will affect your horse. A calm and happy horse reflects a good driver, while a nervous or bad loader or traveller reflects a bad driver.

If you have never towed a horse trailer before or driven a box, the first time to do so is not on the morning of a show. Have a few practice runs first, without a horse on board, until you

Horse and rider correctly dressed for cross country.

are confident enough to give your horse a good, safe journey.

HANDLING HORSES AT EVENTS

It is your responsibility to ensure your horse does not cause any damage to other horses, their riders or property while at an event. All the necessary precautions should be taken to avoid this, like not riding behind other horses or riding into a crowd of people.

If you have a horse that is known to kick out, you can warn other riders and spectators by putting a red ribbon on its tail. Similarly, a horse which is young and unpredictable or excitable should wear a green ribbon on its tail, although taking these precautions does not lessen your responsibility.

RIDER SAFETY

We have already discussed correct riding clothes in Chapter 5, but there is another essential item which should be worn when in competition,

A body protector.

namely a body protector. This should be worn especially when jumping, as its role is to provide padding in order to reduce the degree of injury sustained to internal organs from a fall. As spinal injuries usually result from a twisting motion rather than from a direct blow, a body protector cannot prevent damage to the spine, however.

There are now body protector standards, which have been introduced by the British Equestrian Trade Association (BETA). When choosing a body protector you should ensure it has a shock absorption of at least level 5 (blue label) and preferably of level 7 (red label). It should cover your torso from collar bone to hip bone, both front and back. There is a variety of designs available on the market, some with added features, so there is sure to be one that will suit your budget, taste and competitive discipline.

THE RIGHT TACK AND EQUIPMENT FOR THE JOB

Whatever tack you use in competition make doubly sure that it is safe and secure. Check it before you come away from home and again while tacking up at the event. Not only can a broken rein or girth cost you the competition, but it may also cause you a very serious injury.

To protect you and your horse, use an overgirth when jumping or riding a cross country event, as this will hold the saddle in place should the normal girth give way under strain. Your horse should also wear boots or bandages to protect its legs if it knocks a fence.

COURSE WALKING – A TIME FOR STUDY

When you walk a course, whether it is in a show jumping ring or across country, you should study every fence. The size and width of the fences are important, but so are the approach and landing. Check to see if the ground is wet, and so likely to be churned up by the time you get there. Also check whether any stones or flints have crept on to the track and be sure to throw them well clear. Always walk a cross country course in wellingtons, as you never know if there is going to be a water jump. It is not enough simply to look at it. You will need to step in to see how deep it is and whether the bottom is gravelled or sandy. These factors will determine how you will ride the fence.

Your first impression of any fence will be your horse's only impression, so you owe it to the horse to know what you are asking it to do. If you are asking your horse to trust you to jump fences it might be a little wary of, you should know that it is perfectly safe and within its capabilities. You will know on approach whether there is a ditch on the other side of a fence or how deep the water is, and can ride accordingly. Unless you take the time to check the fences and terrain, you are risking both your own and your horse's safety.

When course-walking, study your options carefully.

FALLS AND FALLING

Whenever you compete in a horse sport you should face the possibility that you may have a fall. Of course you can fall off when in the school at home, but falling off over a fence or when travelling at speed is likely to result in far more serious injuries if you are not aware of how you can minimize the danger by falling correctly. Falls can happen unexpectedly and to any rider, however novice or experienced. So while they cannot be avoided, you can put yourself in the best position to reduce the risk of injury.

Having a safe and secure seat while on the flat and over fences may keep you in the saddle if your horse stumbles, preventing you from flying straight over its head. Concentration will also help you to anticipate a fall and try to fall safely or jump clear if the horse is going to fall as well. If your mind is not on the job then you will have no chance to do this.

The biggest problem with falls is not actually the falling off itself, but the fear of falling. Many novice riders can be so conscious of falling that they are not able to relax, and being relaxed is the greatest aid to keeping you in the saddle. If a fearful rider does take a tumble, then their injuries are likely to be far worse than those of a relaxed person because they will stiffen and brace themselves, falling flat, rather than tucking up and rolling.

Many beginners are nervous of falling off and being dragged. However, as long as your stirrups are the right size for you, this is very unlikely.

Learning how to roll up and away from your horse will help to minimize injury.

The problem of course is that falling off is usually the last thing you want to think about, especially when negotiating a tricky fence. However, you should think about falling and what to do in the event of a fall, far in advance of any competitions.

This is what you should do in the event of a fall.

U Roll yourself up and away from your horse. Watch jockeys on the television; many of them fall, but very few are seriously hurt, because they know exactly how to do it.

U Decide when you have reached the point of no return, and allow yourself to fall rather than

clinging on. If you cling on you may panic the horse or get trampled if you then slide between its legs.

U Do not put out your hand in an attempt to break your fall, as you will only end up breaking your arm. Aim to fall on your shoulder and roll.

U Protect your arms and legs, and in the process your internal organs, by tucking them in immediately you feel yourself go.

U Let your reins go, unless by doing so you risk further accidents (if you are on a busy road, for example). By holding on to the

How not to do it. Decide when is the point of no return and try to jump free, letting go of the reins and tucking into a ball.

reins you may be dragged or get trampled on, or you may dislocate your shoulder and damage your horse's mouth.

U If you feel all right and have been passed by the emergency services at a competition, check that your horse has not sustained any injury. Feel its legs to make sure there is no swelling and look for any cuts.

U If the horse is lame, walk it slowly back to the horsebox and get the vet on call to look at it.

U Do remount as soon as possible if you or your horse is not seriously hurt, or suffering from

concussion, otherwise you will lose confidence rapidly as the shock of what has happened starts to dawn on you.

U If you are in pain, out of breath or suspect something is broken do not move and do not let anyone take your hat off until the emergency services arrive.

U Allow the emergency services to take care of you and do not insist on running off to catch your horse, as there will be many people at a competition who will catch your horse for you.

The best advice you can be given is don't expect a fall to occur, but be prepared for one if it does!

RULES AND REGULATIONS

The main rules concerning competitions are those set by the various governing bodies on correct dress and tack. Every show now insists that anyone mounted while on the showground must wear a riding hat. Many ruling bodies also stipulate that such a hat must be of current BSI standard with a three-point harness. The Pony Club has led the way on this issue, and all members riding at Pony Club events must have correct and safe riding clothes.

When competing in official BHS horse trials you must wear a body protector and a BS4472 skull cap with cover. The British Show Jumping Association (BSJA) recommends BS standard hats, but has not yet made them mandatory. When showing, many county shows now insist that BS standard riding hats are worn, and in any event BS6473 or BS4472 are now compulsory for the jumping phase of working hunter classes.

INSURANCE

If you compete, in whatever category, you should have some sort of personal insurance policy for yourself. While the horse you are riding will probably be insured against accident and injury, you might not be. If the horse you are riding is not your own, check with the horse's owner to see whether you are covered. In any event it is a sensible idea to take out personal insurance that covers you when riding in competition, whether on your own horse or not.

CHAPTER 9

CRIME PREVENTION

STABLE/FIELD SECURITY

Horse thieves are not selective in the animals they steal. They have no interest in whether the horse is a much loved family pet or a top show-jumper. To them the horse is money and they will take it any way they can.

Horses in fields need protection. First, the field gate should be padlocked at both ends (with current BSI locks), otherwise thieves will simply lift the gate off its hinges.

You can also buy alarm systems which will go off if the gate is opened. If the gate leads out on to a public road, try to resite it if possible where it is in view of some houses or the yard.

Horses are also just as likely to be taken from their stables. Thieves have been known to bring their own straw and lay it down across the yard so there is no noise.

Alarms can be put on to individual stable doors or on to the yard gate, so that if either is opened the alarm will go off.

Any horseowner should be aware that stealing horses is big business. Thieves no longer come upon horses by chance and decide to take them; the whole thing is planned in

Padlock gates at both ends and turn the top hinge upside down to prevent the gate from being lifted clean off its hinges.

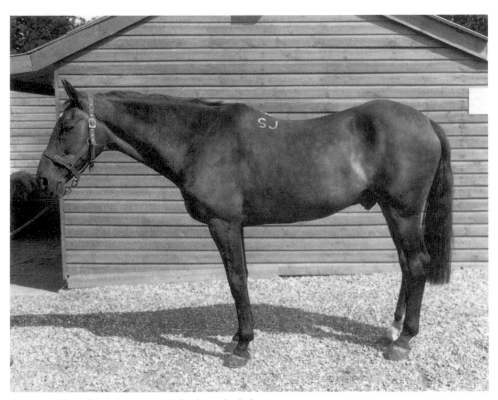

An owner's initials freeze-marked on their horse.

advance, and thieves often steal to order, scouring the countryside for a horse for which they know they have a buyer. You therefore have to make it as difficult for the thieves to steal your horses as possible.

As well as your regular maintenance visits, try also to visit your horse as early in the morning and as late at night as possible, and try to vary the times of these visits so there is no set pattern. Security lighting will also deter thieves. A passive infrared detector will be invisible to the thieves until they walk through the detector beam, when the floodlights will switch on. This is much safer and better for your horse than leaving floodlights on all night.

A crime prevention officer, who can be contacted through your local police station, will be only too pleased to offer you advice on securing your premises.

HORSE AND TACK THEFT – DETERRENTS

The best-known deterrent is freeze-marking. This was pioneered by MMB Farmkey in 1987. A super-chilled marker is applied to a clipped area of the horse on the left side of the saddle patch. This kills the pigment cells in the hair, which regrows white within a few weeks. Grey or lighter animals can also be marked using the same method, but the mark produced remains bald.

These marks are usually placed on the shoulder for ease of identification.

MMB Farmkey has the sole authorization for the maintenance of a National Security Register. The information contained in the register is available to police forces throughout the country, seven days a week, 24 hours a day, to assist in tracing lost or stolen horses. There are other freeze-marking companies, although you need to choose one that has a comprehensive register and back-up service.

Many insurance companies offer premium reductions if your horse is freeze-marked.

Other deterrents involve hoof branding, where the farrier burns an identification code (often the owner's postcode) into the horse's hooves. It is painless but not permanent so has to be done twice a year.

Hoof branding.

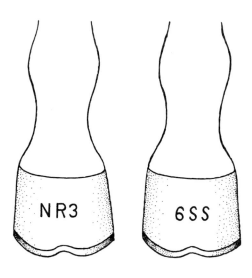

Identichipping is another means of identifying horses. A small chip, the size of a grain of rice, is injected under the horse's skin by a vet. While there is no visible sign, it will help in identification, as it will be detected when a special scanner is used. A scanner network, set up by animalcare, has been spread across major sales rings, as well as slaughter houses where meat is sold for human consumption. Horsewatch co-ordinators and crime prevention officers (see page 93) are also aware of this method of identifying stolen horses, and scanners are supplied on a free loan basis to establishments or personnel who require them for the possible identification of lost or stolen horses.

IDENTIFICATION

Everything you own relating to your horse should be identifiable as yours. This not only means your horse and tack, but your horsebox or trailer as well. In the event of recovery of stolen goods you will be reunited with your possessions far more quickly.

You should fill in a description chart showing your horse's markings, which should also include such things as scars, whorls and any other distinguishing marks. Taking colour photographs of your horse from both sides, and from front and rear, is an excellent idea. While a police officer may not be able to tell what a white blaze on a horse's face should look like, with a picture the officer can match marks up exactly. Also remember to include the hooves in

Opposite: *Identification diagram.*

Registration No _____ (for office use only)

Outline Diagram

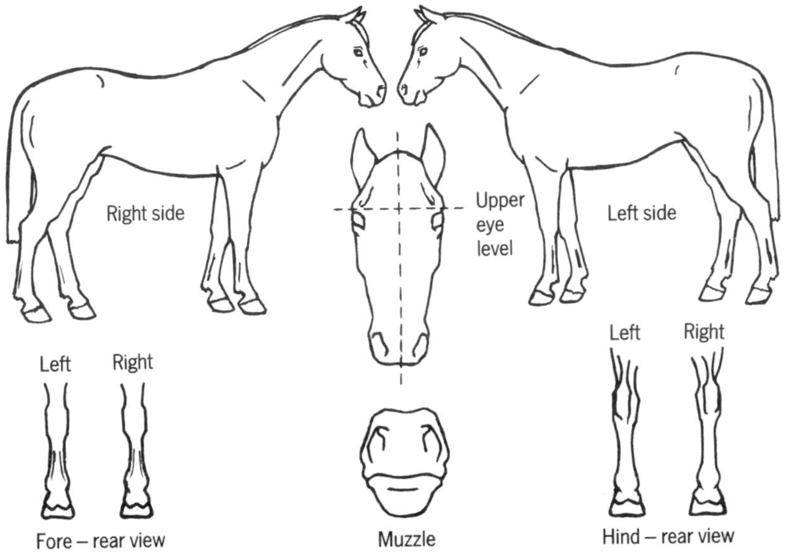

Right side
Upper eye level
Left side

Left   Right

Left   Right

Fore – rear view

Muzzle

Hind – rear view

Name _____ Sex _____ Age _____

Colour _____ Breed/Type _____ Height _____

Owner's name _____

Address _____

_____

Telephone: (Day) _____ (Evening) _____

Where horse/pony is stabled or turned out _____

_____

Stable Telephone _____

Horse's/pony's distinguishing marks _____

_____

_____

Freeze-mark, hoof brand or microchip? Yes/No Number _____

your photographs, as white or dark hooves offer further points of identification. When taking pictures, take one set in the summer and another in the winter, as the same horse can look very different as the seasons change.

Trailers

You may be able to obtain a discount from your insurers if your trailer or horsebox is security-marked. However, here is a word of caution about trailer insurance: check with your insurers whether your trailer is covered if it is not kept in a locked building (even with an anti-theft device fitted). Many insurance policies do not cover it unless it is, even though most trailers are kept outside. If the insurance company which insures your horse will not insure your trailer when out of a locked building and you wish to keep it outside, you may have to insure it separately with another insurer.

A wheel clamp is a good method of securing a trailer or horsebox.

Tack

Tack can also be identichipped or marked with your postcode, by means of metal identity punches. Again, you should also take photographs so that there can be no confusion over identity.

ENLISTING HELP

To help in the fight against equestrian crime you can ask your friends and neighbours to help. If you are away, let them know and ask them to keep a look-out for you. If they suspect anything and cannot contact you, tell them to call the police immediately.

There is now a specialist equestrian crime unit at the Metropolitan Police Mounted Division headquarters, based at Imber Court in London.

As thieves often have a wide network, the crime unit can liaise with other police forces.

WHAT TO DO IF YOUR HORSE/TACK IS STOLEN

Speed is absolutely vital if you are to have the greatest chance of recovery. Always telephone the police and make local enquiries to see if anyone saw or heard anything suspicious. If your horse is freeze-marked let the company know so it can alert auctioneers and ports. You should also do the following.

ᴜ Ask the police to arrange for sales in other areas to be checked.

ᴜ Check auctions being held the next day or in that week, as thieves often steal a horse they have had their eye on the night before, having already booked it into a sale.

ᴜ Telephone local slaughter houses and give them a description of your horse.

ᴜ Keep on checking sales, if possible up and down the country. The BHS will supply you with a list of sales and auctions if you send them a large stamped addressed envelope.

ᴜ Ask trade magazines and local newspapers if they will publish news of the theft.

ᴜ Inform radio stations and ask them to broadcast the message, giving a description of your horse.

ᴜ Put up posters and details in riding schools and livery yards, and in saddlers wherever you can.

ᴜ Inform your insurers, who will need to know that your horse has been stolen and may provide you with recovery expenses.

HORSEWATCH SCHEMES

Many horseowners throughout Britain are determined to help the police crack equestrian crime. Every week more and more people decide to join Horsewatch schemes, and if one is not operating in their area they set one up of their own. Similar to the Neighbourhood Watch schemes, Horsewatch members aim to report anything suspicious and to pass on any information that comes their way. As the system grows, a national network may prove to be a major force in the fight against horse and tack thieves.

The first Horsewatch scheme was set up in 1989 and the idea has grown rapidly. Every Horsewatch group is set up with the assistance of its local crime prevention officer. Each group is led by a co-ordinator who is contacted as soon as there is any news about thefts or information about stolen horses.

The BHS has produced a very comprehensive booklet entitled *How to Set up a Horsewatch*, which is free to anyone who sends a stamped addressed envelope.

CRIMES OF CRUELTY

Many of us will have seen a horse at some time or other being cruelly treated, or at least we believe it to be so. Cruelty can range from beating or whipping a horse to starving it or making it jump fences time and time again when the horse is clearly incapable of doing so.

The Protection of Animals Act 1911 (England and Wales) and the Protection of Animals Act 1912 (Scotland) list many offences, and if a person is found to have committed any of them or has permitted anyone else to commit them, they will be held liable for their actions in law.

An owner or keeper will also be offending if he or she fails to feed the horse, to slaughter the horse should this be necessary to prevent unnecessary suffering, or to ensure the horse receives veterinary attention if needed.

However, inflicting pain does not constitute an offence if it was deemed to be necessary. In other words, cruelty can be defined as causing unnecessary suffering. For instance, if an owner administers an injurious drug or attempts to poison the horse, he or she will be causing unnecessary suffering. However, if a horse falls into a water-filled ditch out on a ride and there is no help available, the rider may whip and shout at the horse in an attempt to make it jump out of the ditch and so prevent it from drowning. The rider may have inflicted both physical and mental pain, but in doing so may have saved the horse's life.

What should you do then if you pass a horse every day to and from work, and you see that it is continually tethered in the same spot, without water? Or what if you have your suspicions that a neighbouring yard is using painful methods to train their horses in order to sell them on as quickly as possible? First, do not interfere yourself, or you may alert the possible offenders, or put yourself in danger, or you may be wrong. What you should do is report such incidents to the RSPCA or your local BHS Welfare Officer, who will investigate the matter promptly and take all necessary action. You should be vigilant for all horses' sake, but by interfering you could make the matter ten times worse.

Remember, you should do all that you can to ensure a high standard of living for the horse, and in the interests of safety, you should endeavour to learn to look after and ride it competently, but that any such care or riding should be carried out within the law.

INDEX

Page numbers in *italic* refer to the illustrations